Teacher's Handbook

Levels 1–2

Hazel Geatches, Series Editor

Great Clarendon Street, Oxford, OX2 6DP, United Kingdom

Oxford University Press is a department of the University of Oxford. It furthers the University's objective of excellence in research, scholarship, and education by publishing worldwide. Oxford is a registered trade mark of Oxford University Press in the UK and in certain other countries

First published in 2013
2018 2017 2016
10 9 8 7 6 5 4 3 2

ISBN: 978 0 19 464647 5

Printed in China

This book is printed on paper from certified and well-managed sources

ACKNOWLEDGEMENTS

The Publisher and Series Editor would like to thank John Clegg (CLIL Adviser) and Robert Quinn (Teaching Notes Adviser) for their input.

Contents

Level 1

Level 2

Introduction

About Oxford Read and Discover

Oxford Read and Discover is a series of graded Readers from Levels 1 to 6, suitable for students of English from age six and older. The levels have been designed to match the language content of Elementary English language coursebooks from Grades 1 to 6.

These reading books provide a wide variety of non-fiction topics that can be used for cross-curricular work or for Content and Language Integrated Learning (CLIL). The topics have been chosen to stimulate students' interest and to cover key curriculum content from three broad subject areas: The World of Science and Technology, The Natural World, and The World of Arts and Social Studies.

Oxford Read and Discover combines lively reading material with carefully graded language, enabling students to discover more about the world while learning English at the same time. See the series chart on page 32 and the contents summary chart on pages 6–7. Or go to **www.oup.com/elt/teacher/readanddiscover**

Series Components, Levels 1–2

Reader

Each Reader provides carefully structured and supported **reading text** about an engaging topic. The following features support the development of general reading skills.

- The **contents page** and **introduction page** at the beginning of the Reader prepare students for what they will read in the chapters.
- The **reading text** is organized into **chapters**, each with a **heading**. The text is accompanied by **photos**, **illustrations**, and **diagrams**, to stimulate interest and support understanding, and **labels** are included for key language and concepts. There are also **Discover! fact boxes** and **cartoons**, to further stimulate interest.

At the back of each Reader the following are provided.

- In Level 1, a page of **activities** for each chapter. In Level 2, two pages of **activities** for each chapter. These activities are carefully graded and are based on the language and content of the chapter. They are designed to support the development of a range of reading and writing skills, as well as general cognitive skills and critical thinking skills. The activities can be done after each chapter, or after the whole Reader has been read. There is a very clear reference to the activities pages in each chapter.
- Two **project pages** that provide extension material, encouraging students to personalize the topic, or research the topic further. Structured support is provided for these activities.
- To support the development of dictionary skills, there is a **picture dictionary** for key vocabulary that is likely to be new.

Audio CD

An Audio CD accompanies each Reader, and provides a recording of the text in both American and British English.

Activity Book

An Activity Book is available for each Reader, providing additional reading and writing practice for each chapter, as well as consolidation activities, Picture Dictionary revision, and a book review page. Activity Book answers are available on the Teacher's Website at **www.oup.com/elt/teacher/readanddiscover**

Teacher's Handbook Levels 1–2

This Teacher's Handbook outlines the methodology of the **Oxford Read and Discover** series, and provides an overview of the Readers at Levels 1–2, to help with lesson planning. There are **general teaching suggestions** that you can adapt to specific Readers and teaching contexts, and there are some ideas on using the **photocopiable world map** provided on page 9. **CLIL guidance** notes are also provided on page 10.

There is a page of **specific teaching notes** for each Reader, providing a summary of topics, curriculum links, main vocabulary and grammar, as well as **answers** to the Reader activities. **Specific teaching ideas** are also provided, including opportunities for speaking practice. Look out for the READ & TALK ideas!

Teacher's Website

This Teacher's Handbook and the Activity Book answers are available on the Teacher's Website at **www.oup.com/elt/teacher/readanddiscover**

Oxford Read and Discover • Contents Summary, Level 1

Subject Area	Reader Title	Main Vocabulary For full list see teaching notes for each Reader	Grammar	Main Topics For full list see teaching notes for each Reader	Curriculum Links
1 The World of Science & Technology	Eyes	animals; parts of the body; places; sizes; colors; numbers	present simple; *can/can't*; question forms; imperative; adjectives; prepositions; adverbs	parts of an eye; parts of the body; animals; food; protecting eyes; sizes; light and color; night and day	Civics; Mathematics; Science
	Fruit	fruit; animals; parts of fruit; food and drink; shapes; sizes; colors; weather; daily activities	present simple; *can/can't*; question forms; imperative; adjectives; prepositions	types of fruit; the life cycle of a fruit plant; parts of a plant; plants and animals; weather and climate; fruit and drink; how to eat fruit; uses and benefits of fruit; shapes; sizes and measurements	Civics; Mathematics; Science
	Trees	places; parts of a tree; weather; fruit; materials; animals; countries; numbers; sizes	present simple; *can/can't*; question forms; imperative; adjectives; prepositions	parts of a tree; types of tree; life cycle of a tree; carbon dioxide and oxygen; weather and climate; what we get from trees; animals and trees; how to protect trees; sizes, measurements, and quantities	Civics; Mathematics; Science; Technology
	Wheels	transportation; food; shapes; sizes; daily activities; sports; parts of the body; materials; places; numbers; directions	present simple; *can/can't*; question forms; imperative; adjectives; prepositions; adverbs	machines; materials; daily life; transportation; sports and other hobbies; disabilities; food; electricity; shapes; sizes, measurements, and quantities	Civics; Mathematics; Science; Technology
The Natural World	At the Beach	animals; parts of the body; places; food; sports; sizes; colors; numbers; plants; measurements	present simple; *can/can't*; question forms; imperative; adjectives; prepositions;	physical features of the beach; plants and animals; food chains; parts of the body; camouflage; safety at the beach; materials	Civics; Geography; Science
	In the Sky	transportation; weather; places; colors; shapes; sizes; numbers	present simple; *can/can't*; question forms; imperative; adjectives; prepositions	the sky and space; moons, stars, and planets; day and night; machines; light and energy; electricity; weather; space travel; shapes; sizes and measurements	Geography; Mathematics; Science; Technology
	Wild Cats	animals; places; parts of the body; food and drink; colors; numbers; sizes	present simple; *can/can't*; question forms; imperative; adjectives; prepositions; adverbs	types of wild cat; climate; parts of a cat's body; where wild cats live; senses; what wild cats eat; baby wild cats and parents; wild cats in danger; sizes and measurements	Civics; Geography; Mathematics; Science
	Young Animals	daily activities; parts of the body; weather; sizes; transportation; clothes; numbers	present simple; *can/can't*; question forms; imperative; adjectives; prepositions; adverbs	parts of the body; what your body can do; senses; sports and exercise; daily life; protecting your body; healthy food; quantities and measurements	Civics; Mathematics; Science
The World of Arts & Social Studies	Art	types of art; places; countries; parts of the body; artist's equipment; materials; animals; shapes; sizes; colors; weather; numbers	present simple; *can/can't*; question forms; imperative; adjectives; prepositions	types of art; lines and shapes; places and countries; animals; materials; tools; museums	Art; Civics; Mathematics; Science; Technology
	Schools	buildings; places; transportation; school equipment; food; clothes; animals; weather; age; sizes; colors; countries	present simple; *can/can't*; question forms; imperative; adjectives; prepositions;	daily life; places and countries; classroom behaviour; uniform; sports and other hobbies; food; weather; sizes	Civics; Geography; Mathematics; Science

Oxford Read and Discover • Contents Summary, Level 2

Subject Area	Reader Title	Main Vocabulary For full list see teaching notes for each Reader	Grammar	Main Topics For full list see teaching notes for each Reader	Curriculum Links
The World of Science & Technology	Electricity	household objects; places; daily activities; transportation; machines; materials; sizes; colors	present simple; *can/can't*; question forms; imperative; adjectives; prepositions	daily life; machines; electricity in nature; how we make electricity; batteries; how we get electricity; how electricity moves through materials; pollution; being safe with electricity; uses of electricity	Civics; Science
	Plastic	household objects; toys; materials; places; food and drink; daily activities; transportation; parts of a house; sizes; colors	present simple; *can/can't*; question forms; imperative; adjectives; prepositions	plastic things; types of plastic; how we make plastic; daily life; plastic at home; plastic waste; how plastic can hurt animals; recycling plastic; making plastic from plants	Civics; Science; Technology
	Sunny and Rainy	weather; seasons; animals; food; colors; numbers; measurements; places; daily activities	present simple; *can/can't*, question forms; imperative; adjectives; prepositions; adverbs	weather; seasons; the water cycle; types of wind; animals; day and night; light and dark; geographical features; states of water; plants and animals	Science
	Your Body	daily activities; parts of the body; weather; sizes; transportation; clothes; numbers	present simple; *can/can't*; question forms; imperative; adjectives; prepositions; adverbs	Parts of the body; what your body can do; senses; sports and exercise; daily life; protecting your body; healthy food; quantities and measurements	Civics; Mathematics; Science
The Natural World	Camouflage	animals; plants; places; parts of the body; sizes; shapes; colors; seasons; weather	present simple; *can/can't*; present continuous; question forms; imperative; adjectives; prepositions; adverbs	animals and their homes; parts of an animal's body; shapes; plants; seasons; weather and climate	Mathematics; Science
	Earth	transportation; places; animals; weather; countries; seasons; numbers	present simple; *can/can't*, question forms; imperative; adjectives; prepositions; adverbs	places and countries; physical features of Earth; land and water; weather and climate; plants and animals; time and measurements	Geography; Mathematics; Science
	Farms	places; weather; seasons; animals; food; clothes; sizes; numbers	present simple; *can/can't*; present continuous; question forms; imperative; adjectives; prepositions; adverbs	types of farms; animals and animal products; plants and crops; food; machines; weather; sizes, measurements, and quantities	Geography; Mathematics; Science; Technology
	In the Mountains	places; food and drink; animals; parts of the body; plants; sports; transportation; sizes; shapes; weather; seasons; continents	present simple; *can/can't*; question forms; imperative; adjectives; prepositions; adverbs	how mountains form; volcanoes; living in the mountains; animals; plants; ice and snow; climate and countries; weather and seasons; mountain sports; safety in the mountains; sizes and measurements	Civics; Geography; Mathematics; Science; Technology
The World of Arts & Social Studies	Cities	places; buildings; transportation; time; jobs; sizes; numbers	present simple; *can/can't*; present continuous; question forms; imperative; adjectives; prepositions	cities and countries; places in cities; buildings and homes; daily life; tourism; transportation; jobs; time; sizes, measurements, and quantities	Civics; Geography; Mathematics; Technology
	Jobs	jobs; places; colors; clothes; transportation; food; animals; parts of a house; household objects; seasons	present simple; *can/can't*; present continuous; question forms; imperatives; adjectives; prepositions	types of job; where people work; when people work; making things; helping people; working with animals; jobs with animals	Civics; Science; Technology

Using Oxford Read and Discover Levels 1–2

Oxford Read and Discover is designed to develop reading, writing, listening, and speaking skills, as well as general critical thinking skills. The Readers can be used in a number of ways, with individuals or with a whole class. With a whole class, you have the option of using the same Reader with all students, or allowing your students to read independently, choosing different titles at different levels. How you use the Readers will depend on the teaching context and linguistic and cognitive abilities of your students. You can adapt the general teaching suggestions below to suit your needs.

Reading Skills

The main goal of the Readers is to provide opportunities for intensive and extensive reading practice. Students can read intensively, making use of the activities for each chapter at the back of the book as an integrated part of reading. They can do the relevant activities after reading each chapter, or they can do all the activities after finishing the whole Reader.

Students can also use the Readers for extensive practice, reading independently for pleasure. This approach is particularly suitable for students with higher levels of English, or even bilingual students. You may want them to work on Readers in a particular order, or you can allow them to explore the topics in their own order of preference. Encourage students to keep track of the Readers that they have completed.

Writing Skills

The activities at the back of the Reader provide integrated reading and writing practice, with a variety of activity types at word and sentence level, such as matching, labelling, completing sentences, circling the correct words, true/false sentences, answering questions, ordering words, puzzles, and providing personal responses.

The projects provide further opportunities for reading and writing. Students can also explore topics in other books or on the Internet, and they can present their findings, for example, as posters, fact boxes, charts, or summaries.

For further reading and writing practice, give students sections of text with key words removed or changed, and ask them to complete or correct the text. You can also give students key words from the picture dictionary and ask them to write sentences with the words. Students can then create their own versions, and test other students.

The Activity Books provide additional reading and writing practice.

Listening and Speaking Skills

To develop listening skills, the texts are recorded onto Audio CD. You can choose between American and British English:

	Level 1	Level 2
American English	tracks 1–8	tracks 1–8
British English	tracks 9–16	tracks 9–16

To raise their awareness of pronunciation and intonation, students can listen to the Audio CD as they read.

For active practice of pronunciation and intonation, students can listen and read out loud at the same time, or pause the Audio CD after paragraphs and repeat what they heard. Students can then listen to the Audio CD after they have read each chapter or the whole book, with their books open or closed.

For active listening practice, give students sections of text with key words removed or changed, and ask them to complete or correct the texts while listening.

For speaking practice, use the questions on the introduction page of the Reader (page 3) to engage students in discussion before reading. You can also build on these questions to stimulate discussion after students have read the Reader.

Some of the projects also provide an opportunity to develop simple listening and speaking skills, for example, with surveys and presentations. See also the After Reading ideas on page 9, and look out for the READ & TALK ideas in the teaching notes for each Reader.

Critical Thinking Skills

The Readers in this series help to develop critical thinking skills, as students need not only to understand English, but also to process topic information. The activities provide practice of both the language and content of the Reader, and they develop students' critical thinking skills with activities such as organizing information into charts, sequencing or correcting information, solving puzzles, giving personal opinions, writing notes, and planning projects.

Individual Use

If a Reader is read by one student only, the student can work at his/her own pace. You can check their understanding by asking simple questions, for example: *What is your favorite chapter / page / picture?* If the student is also doing the activities, you can also check these orally.

Some of the projects ask students to work with others. If a student is not working with a whole class on the same Reader, he/she may be able to talk to other class members to do the project. Otherwise he/she can ask friends or members of the family, or you can work with the student. Students may want to do this in their first language, but you can then help them to present their findings in English.

Whole-Class Use

If a whole class is reading the same Reader, you can use some of the Before Reading and After Reading ideas on page 9. Some projects provide good opportunities for whole-class activities, for example, class surveys. Some ideas are provided in the teaching notes for each Reader. You can also use the After Reading ideas on page 9.

Before Reading

If you are working with the whole class, you can introduce the topic, check on previous knowledge, and stimulate students' interest with the following activities.

- Show the cover, initially hiding the title, and ask students what they think the book is about, and what they already know about the topic, for example: *What is the title of this book? What is this book about? What do you know about [eyes / young animals]?*
- Ask students what vocabulary they know about the topic, and ask them to guess what vocabulary will be in the Reader. You can write all the vocabulary on the board, and also introduce any key vocabulary from the picture dictionary that you think students will need. Or you can leave students to find the new vocabulary at the back of the Reader when they need it.
- Use the photos and questions on the introduction page of the Reader (page 3) to stimulate discussion and thought.

- If the Reader includes content from around the world, you can use the ideas and the world map below.
- Before each chapter, ask students about the photos and illustrations, for example: *What can you see? Where is the [monkey]? What is it doing?*

After Reading

After each chapter or after the whole Reader has been read, check how much students have understood and provide opportunities for revision and further practice with the following activities, as a whole class or in pairs. In a mixed-ability class, you might prefer the students to read at their own pace, and then go straight to the activities when they are ready. You can then check students' understanding once they have all finished. If you check answers orally, students can practice their listening skills.

- Say or write sentences about the topic and ask students to say or write if they are true or false.
- Ask or write general comprehension questions.
- Describe something from the Reader without saying its name; ask students to guess what it is, or ask them to ask questions and only answer yes or no.
- Depending on their level, ask students to say or write three, five, or ten new things that they have learned.
- Ask students what their favorite Discover! fact is.
- If students are reading different Readers, ask them to present their Reader to the rest of the class, for example: *The name of the book is ...; It's about ...; My favorite chapter is ...; My favorite page is ...; My favorite picture is ...*
- Some projects at the back of the Reader provide opportunities for students to explore or personalize the topic. There are also opportunities for whole-class speaking practice, for example, with surveys.
- The picture dictionary is a great resource for practice of key vocabulary after reading. Show or say the words and ask students to match them to the pictures, or show the pictures and ask students to say or write the words.

Using the World Map

Oxford Read and Discover provides very international, global content, and many of the Readers refer to places all around the world. It is important that students know where key places are, to ensure full understanding of the text. You can use your own maps, atlas, or globe, but to support you and your students, a photocopiable world map is provided below. The map is blank and only has the continents marked, to provide maximum flexibility – the amount of detail that you or your students add will depend on the Reader, the activity, and the age and level of your students.

Here are some ideas.

- On a copy of the map, mark all the places mentioned in the Reader. Give students a copy of the map to refer to while they read. And/Or after reading, give students a copy of the map and ask them to talk about information that they have learned about these places.
- After reading, give students a copy of the blank map. Ask them to find all the places mentioned in the Reader and to mark them on the map. Then they can add information that they have learned about these places.
- After reading, students can use a copy of the map (blank or with places marked) to accompany a presentation.

Hazel Geatches, Series Editor

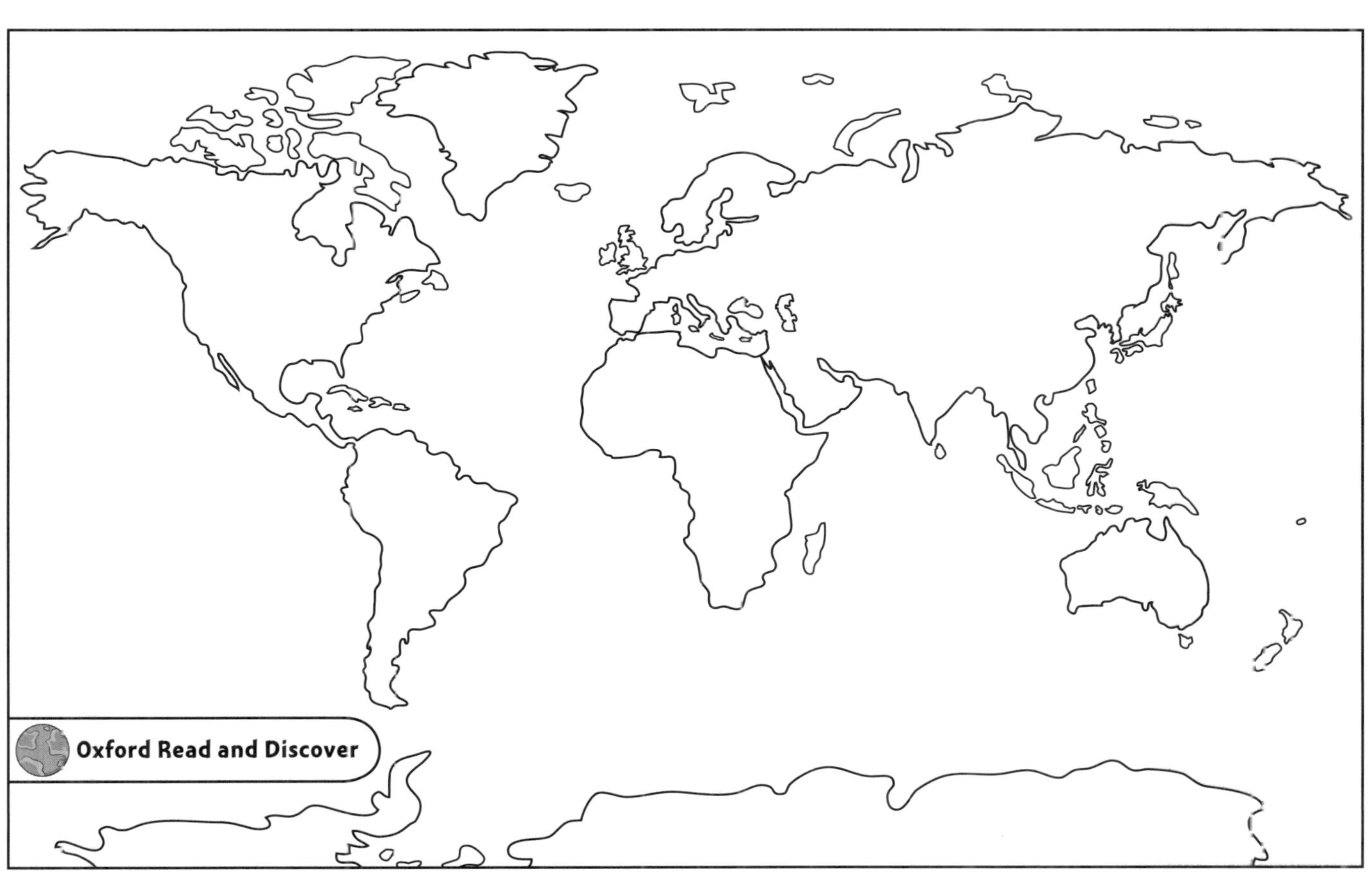

CLIL Guidance

Learning other subjects through English, or CLIL, is a key feature of the **Oxford Read and Discover** series of graded Readers.

What is CLIL?

CLIL stands for 'Content and Language Integrated Learning' and it links learning subjects with language learning. This helps students to develop both language abilities and subject concepts in the second language. It motivates them to use the language: interesting topics encourage students to read, use, and learn English. Also, CLIL builds on the subject knowledge that students have gained using their first language. Once they have learned about a topic in their first language, it is easier for them to read about it in English; and they can expand their understanding of it in English. To help students to do this, CLIL uses a methodology that makes school subjects accessible to students who may be at an early stage in language learning.

CLIL and Oxford Read and Discover

You can see this methodology at work in the **Oxford Read and Discover** series. The language is carefully graded, plenty of visuals make concepts easy to understand, and the activities are designed to help students to use English and learn about the topic at the same time.

The Readers emphasize reading skills, but they also encourage students to write, talk, and listen to the text or to each other. They highlight vocabulary that is specific to the topic, but they also give students practice in organizing and expressing their ideas and opinions about the topic using simple sentences. They focus on language skills, but also on the skills of thinking and processing information that are required in the study of school subjects, and that the students are developing in their first language.

Because the **Oxford Read and Discover** series combines language with content, the Readers can be used by either subject or language teachers.

For Subject Teachers

Some subject teachers are also English teachers. They like to link the work they do on a subject in the students' first language with their English language lessons. The Readers allow them to do this by reinforcing students' knowledge of specific school topics and developing their English language skills at the same time. Alternatively the subject teacher may collaborate with an English teacher and plan a short coordinated scheme of work on a common topic. The subject teacher leads the teaching of the topic in the first language, and the English teacher reinforces it by using a Reader.

Subject teachers teach a lot of information-processing skills that their subject requires, such as using charts, graphs, and maps, searching for information on the Internet, and presenting information in visual and verbal forms. The **Oxford Read and Discover** series makes use of similar skills; the Readers ask students to construct and interpret graphs and charts, to use the Internet to explore topics, to do surveys, make notes, plan, and make simple presentations. Subject teachers who also teach English can easily reinforce the information skills they teach in the first language by using these Readers, because they develop the same skills in English. They can also plan collaborative projects with an English teacher, to focus on a common topic, and on common information and learning skills.

For Language Teachers

Many language teachers nowadays like to expand their language teaching to include some work on other subjects in the curriculum. The **Oxford Read and Discover** series helps them to do this by making these topics available to students whose English language ability is still at a developing stage. The graded language of the texts, the visuals and the supportive activities allow the language teacher to reinforce language development by expanding into a subject without making inappropriate demands on the English language ability of the students.

Students with early levels of English language ability will find it easier to do some activities in their first language, such as surveys, Internet searches, constructing graphs, etc. However, language teachers can help students to talk or write about the results of their activity in English, by providing them with useful vocabulary, sentence starters, etc. The teaching ideas for each Reader often contain examples of sentence starters which will help students do this.

The Readers can also reinforce language that the teacher may be focussing on in an English language coursebook, such as specific grammatical structures or vocabulary. The chart shows which aspects of language are highlighted by each Reader. English teachers can choose to link the language work they may be doing in an English language coursebook with a particular Reader that focusses on similar language.

John Clegg, CLIL Adviser

Teaching Notes

Levels 1–2

Teaching notes for each Reader at Levels 1–2,
including ideas for classroom use
and answers to the activities in the Reader

Eyes

Subject Area

The World of Science & Technology

Topics & Curriculum Links

parts of an eye (Science)
parts of the body (Science)
animals (Science)
food (Science)
protecting eyes (Science; Civics)
sizes (Mathematics)
light and color (Science)
night and day (Science)

Vocabulary

animals; parts of the body; places; sizes; colors; numbers

Grammar

present simple; *can/can't*, question forms; imperative; adjectives; prepositions; adverbs

Activities Answers

Page 20 **1** **1** crab **2** gecko **3** insects **4** duck **2** **1** look **2** big **3** see **4** top

Page 21 **1** **1** eyelashes **2** eyelid **3** pupil **4** eyeball **5** tears **2** **1** true **2** false **3** false **4** true

Page 22 **1** **1** hawk **2** monkey **3** hunt **4** owl **5** jump **2** **1** The hawk can fly fast. **2** People have eyes at the front of their head. **3** The monkey can jump from tree to tree. **4** Some owls can turn their head around.

Page 23 **1** **1** stalk-eyed fly **2** hammerhead shark **3** chameleon **4** frog **2** **1** flat **2** head **3** two **4** can

Page 24 **1** **1** true **2** false **3** true **4** false **2** **1** seal **2** flatfish **3** eyes **4** ocean **5** land **6** water

Page 25 **1** **1** pupils **2** dark **3** lights **4** dogs

Page 26 **1** **1** dragonfly **2** spider **3** scallop **2** **1** six or eight **2** more than 50 **3** thousands **3** **1** insects **2** animals **3** big **4** eyes **5** little **6** many

Page 27 **1** **1** sand **2** desert **3** sunglasses **4** fur **5** windy **6** sunny **2** **1** people – sunglasses **2** meerkats – fur around the eyes **3** camels – long eyelashes

Teaching Ideas

See also pages 8–9 for general ideas that you can adapt. Or go to **www.oup.com/elt/teacher/readanddiscover**

READ & TALK Mystery Eyes

After reading page 3, collect pictures of eyes of typical animals (cow, horse, cat, fish, etc.). Cut out the eyes or cover up everything except the eyes – so that it's not easy to guess which animal it is, as on page 3. Show the eyes to the class and ask students to guess which animal they think it is.

READ & TALK My Eyes Poster

After completing the project, students make a poster about their eyes. They can draw or photograph their eyes and label the parts of the eye. They can also write sentences about their eyes, using page 29 of the Reader for support. Then they present their poster to the rest of the class. Posters can then be displayed together.

READ & TALK Which Animal Is It?

Choose one of the animals in the Reader, and without saying its name, read out one sentence about it and ask students to guess which animals it is. Read out more sentences, one at a time, until students guess the correct animal. Students can then do this in small groups or pairs.

An Animal Eyes Chart

Students work in small groups to make a chart that organizes animal eyes, with four columns labelled: *Name of the Animal*, *Number of Eyes*, *Color of Eyes*, *Place of Eyes*. Students put information for different animals into the chart. They can find pictures of the animals, too. Then they can display the chart and the pictures as a class collage.

Animal Eyes Fact Files

Students write fact files about wild animals or pets that they know. They describe the animals' eyes, using models in the Reader for support, for example: *The [animal] has [number] eyes; It has big/small/[color] eyes; It has eyes at the front/sides of its head/body; It can ...*

Fruit

Subject Area

The World of Science & Technology

Topics & Curriculum Links

types of fruit (Science)
life cycle of a fruit plant (Science)
parts of a plant (Science)
plants and animals (Science)
weather and climate (Science)
food and drink (Science)
how to eat fruit (Civics)
uses and benefits of fruit (Civics)
shapes (Mathematics)
sizes and measurements (Mathematics)

Vocabulary

fruit animals; parts of fruit; food and drink; shapes; sizes; colors; weather; daily activities

Grammar

present simple; *can/can't*; question forms; imperative; adjectives; prepositions

Activities Answers

Page 20 **1** 1 plants 2 Trees 3 fruit 4 grow 5 mango **2** 1 Apples grow on big trees. 2 Some types of fruit grow on little plants. 3 Some fruit plants grow on the ground. 4 Strawberry plants grow on the ground. 5 Kiwi plants are tall and thin.

Page 21 **1** 1 banana 2 apple 3 lemon 4 strawberry 5 orange 6 mango **2** 1 places 2 rainy 3 hot 4 cool 5 grow 6 cool

Page 22 **1** 1 one big seed 2 many little seeds 3 soft fruit 4 hard fruit **2** 1 true 2 true 3 true 4 false 5 false

Page 23 **1** 1 A seed in the fruit makes a new plant. 2 Leaves make food for the new plant so it can grow 3 Flowers grow on the plant. 4 Petals fall from the plant. 5 New fruit grows. 6 Old fruit falls to the ground and rots. **2** 1 flowers 2 petals 3 seeds 4 plants 5 ground 6 leaves

Page 24 **1** 1 fruit 2 bird 3 seeds 4 plants 5 monkey 6 mice **2** 1 new 2 ground 3 plants 4 grow

Page 25 **1** 1 flesh 2 skin 3 seeds **2** 1 peel, flesh 2 wash, skin 3 skin, fruit

Page 26 **1** 1 juice 2 jam 3 pizza 4 olive oil **2** 1 We press fruit to make fruit juice. 2 We use soft fruit to make jam. 3 We use tomatoes to make pizza. 4 We press olives to make olive oil. 5 We use olive oil to cook food.

Page 27 **1** 1 eyes 2 skin 3 walk 4 run 5 grow **2** 1 true 2 true 3 true 4 false 5 false 6 true

Teaching Ideas

See also pages 8–9 for general ideas that you can adapt. Or go to **www.oup.com/elt/teacher/readanddiscover**

READ & TALK A Fruit Survey

After completing the project activity on page 28 of the Reader, students collect the results from the whole class. They can do this by listening to each student giving their information in turn, or by collecting the information in a big version of the chart on page 28 of the Reader. Students then make a class bar graph showing which types of fruit and how much fruit the class ate in a week.

A Fruit Poster

After completing the project activity on page 29 of the Reader, students use their notes to make posters about fruit. Then students can display the posters in class and vote for the best one.

READ & TALK Which Fruit Is It?

Students work in pairs and choose a fruit from the Reader Then they write about it like this, without saying its name: *It's [color]; It's soft/hard. It's long/short/round; It has one seed/many seeds; You (don't) peel the skin; It grows on big trees/little plants/ on the ground.* Then students read out their descriptions and ask the rest of the class to guess which fruit it is.

READ & TALK Food and Drink from Fruit

Students work in small groups and make a chart listing fruit and the types of food and drink you can make from the fruit. They can complete three columns: 'Type of Fruit' 'Food', 'Drink'. Students then share their findings with the class.

Fruit Around the World

Students find out about where fruit grows around the world. They display their findings on a poster with pictures and labels giving the name of the fruit and the countries where the fruit grows. Students can use a copy of the world map on page 9. Posters can then be displayed together.

1 Trees

Subject Area

The World of Science & Technology

Topics & Curriculum Links

parts of a tree (Science)
types of tree (Science)
life cycle of a tree (Science)
carbon dioxide and oxygen (Science)
weather and climate (Science)
what we get from trees (Science; Technology)
animals and trees (Science)
how to protect trees (Science; Civics)
sizes, measurements, and quantities (Mathematics)

Vocabulary

places; parts of a tree; weather; fruit; materials; animals; countries; numbers; sizes

Grammar

present simple; *can/can't*; question forms; imperative; adjectives; prepositions

Activities Answers

Page 20 **1** 1 branches 2 leaves 3 roots 4 trunk **2** 1 plant 2 branches 3 food 4 light 5 year

Page 21 **1** 1 Leaves make food for the tree. 2 Roots take water from the ground. 3 The trunk takes food down the tree and water up the tree. 4 Bark protects the trunk. **2** 1 branches 2 protects 3 air 4 trunk 5 roots

Page 22 **1** 1 big 2 Flowers 3 wind 4 pollen **2** 1 Seeds grow inside fruit. 2 The fruit falls from the tree. 3 The seeds go in the ground. 4 New trees grow.

Page 23 **1** 1 conifers 2 leaves 3 needles 4 broadleaves **2** 1 false 2 false 3 false 4 true 5 true

Page 24 **1** 1 live 2 carbon dioxide 3 good 4 ground 5 ground **2** 1 clean 2 carbon dioxide 3 oxygen 4 rain; sun 5 play

Page 25 **1** 1 rubber 2 wood 3 paper 4 fruit **2** 1 We can make car tyres and many other things with rubber. 2 The trunks and branches of trees give us wood. 3 We make toys, tables, homes, paper, and many other things with wood.

Page 26 **1** 1 snake 2 bird 3 monkey 4 insects **2** 1 Many animals live in trees. 2 Animals can find food in trees. 3 The monkey eats leaves and fruit. 4 The snake lives in a tree.

Page 27 **1** 1 People cut down trees. 2 Little plants grow around tree trunks. 3 Animals eat tree leaves and bark. **2** 1 Some animals, little plants and people are bad for trees. 2 Cars, fires and factories can make the air and rain dirty. 3 Every day people cut down about 10 million trees.

Teaching Ideas

See also pages 8–9 for general ideas that you can adapt. Or go to **www.oup.com/elt/teacher/readanddiscover**

READ & TALK Things from Trees

After reading Chapter 6, students find out more about what things we can get from trees. Students make a list of the things in their home that come from trees, for example, things made from rubber, wood, and paper. They can also make a list of fruit that they eat that comes from trees. Students then share their lists with the class.

Trees Where We Live

After completing the project, students make a collage of different trees that grow where they live. They can take photos or draw pictures of the trees, and then label them, using the names of the trees in English or in their own language. Students can also make a map of a local area, for example, the school grounds, or a local park, and they can show what trees grow in the area. All the collages can then be displayed together.

READ & TALK A Tree Poster

Ask students to take a photo or draw a picture of a tree that grows near where they live. Then they label all the parts of the tree, including any seeds or fruit that the tree produces. They can also bring in leaves and needles that have fallen from the tree. Students then present their tree to the class, by answering the questions on page 28 of the Reader.

READ & TALK A Tree Quiz

Ask the class quiz questions, using facts from the Reader. Ask true/false questions, or questions starting with *What, Where, When*, etc. Students can work in pairs or small groups, and they can look for the answers in the Reader. Then in pairs or small groups, students can ask their own quiz questions.

Trees Around the World

Students choose a tree and find out about where it grows around the world. Then they make a poster showing a picture of the tree, and the countries where the tree grows. Students can use a copy of the world map on page 9 to show the countries where the tree grows. Posters can then be displayed together.

Subject Area

The World of Science & Technology

Topics & Curriculum Links

machines (Science; Technology)
materials (Science; Technology)
daily life (Civics)
transportation (Technology)
sports and other hobbies (Civics)
disabilities (Science; Civics)
food (Science)
electricity (Science)
shapes (Mathematics)
sizes, measurements, and quantities (Mathematics)

Vocabulary

transportation; food; shapes; sizes; daily activities; sports; parts of the body; materials; places; numbers; directions

Grammar

present simple; *can/can't*; question forms; imperative; adjectives; prepositions; adverbs

Activities Answers

Page 20 **1** 1 wheelbarrow 2 bus 3 people 4 roller skates **2** 1 round 2 front 3 big 4 little

Page 21 **1** 1 push 2 sports 3 store 4 wheelchair 5 stroller 6 pull **2** 1 true 2 false 3 true 4 true

Page 22 **1** 1 road 2 helmet 3 pump 4 metal 5 tire **2** 1 You use your legs to turn bicycle wheels. 2 You use a pump to put air into a tire. 3 You wear a helmet to protect your head.

Page 23 **1** 1 plane 2 bicycle 3 train 4 car **2** 1 false 2 true 3 false 4 true

Page 24 **1** 1 left 2 right 3 up 4 down 5 round **2** 1 fairground 2 push 3 sit 4 yo-yo

Page 25 **1** 1 A combine harvester cuts wheat. 2 A pizza cutter cuts pizza. 3 A saw cuts wood. **2** 1 sharp 2 fast 3 wheel 4 cut 5 moves

Page 26 **1** 1 clock 2 roller 3 rolling pin **2** 1 make 2 turn 3 paint 4 long

Page 27 **1** 1 wind turbine 2 river 3 water mill 4 electricity **2** 1 false 2 true 3 true 4 false

Teaching Ideas

See also pages 8–9 for general ideas that you can adapt. Or go to **www.oup.com/elt/teacher/readanddiscover**

READ & TALK Mystery Wheels

After reading page 3, collect pictures of wheels. Cut out the wheels or cover up everything except the wheels – so that it's not easy to guess what type of wheel it is, as on page 3. Show each wheel to the class and ask students to guess what type of wheel they think it is.

READ & TALK A Wheels Collage

After completing the project, students collect more pictures of things that have wheels. They label them. Then they create a class collage of wheels, organizing them into different categories – things with one/two/three/four/ more wheels.

READ & TALK Where is this Wheel?

Choose one of the wheels in the Reader, and without saying its name, read out one sentence about it and ask students to guess where the wheel is. Read out more sentences, one at a time, until students guess the correct wheel. Students can then do this in small groups or pairs.

A Wheel Diary

Students keep a record of all the different wheels that they see at school or around them during a day, or a few days. They can record their wheels in a chart, or in a diagram like the one on page 29 of the Reader, organizing them into different categories – things with one/two/three/four/ more wheels.

READ & TALK A New Machine

Students design a new machine with wheels. First they decide how many wheels it has, if they are big or little, what they are made of, and what the machine can do. Then they draw the machine, and they can talk or write about it like this: *This machine has [number] wheels. The wheels are big/ little. This machine can ...* Students then display all the designs together. They can vote for their favorite design.

Subject Area
The Natural World

Topics & Curriculum Links
physical features of the beach (Geography)
plants and animals (Science)
food chains (Science)
parts of the body (Science)
camouflage (Science)
safety at the beach (Civics)
materials (Science)
measurements (Mathematics)

Vocabulary
animals; plants; parts of the body; places; food; sports; sizes; colors; numbers

Grammar
present simple; *can/can't*; question forms; imperative; adjectives; prepositions

Activities Answers

Page 20 **1** **1** The ocean is salt water. **2** At low tide the ocean goes down the beach. **3** Sand is little pieces of rock and shell. **4** At high tide the ocean goes up the beach. **2** **1** rocks **2** beach **3** shell **4** waves **5** sand Secret word: ocean.

Page 21 **1** **1** The tellin shell hides under the sand. **2** The flat periwinkle hides in seaweed. **3** The barnacle lives on rocks. **2** **1** The tellin shell gets food with a siphon. **2** The barnacle's shell grows onto rocks. **3** Some barnacles grow on whales.

Page 22 **1** **1** rockpool **2** starfish **3** clam **4** crab **2** **1** rockpools **2** claws **3** barnacles **4** stomach **5** clams

Page 23 **1** **1** This is a prawn. The prawn walks with 10 legs, and it swims with 10 legs! **2** (possible answer) This is a seahorse. The seahorse hides in the seaweed. In green seaweed, the seahorse is green, but in yellow seaweed, it's yellow! **2** **1** food **2** little **3** twenty **4** swims **5** green

Page 24 **1** **1** seal **2** dolphin **3** basking shark **2** **1** air **2** head **3** fish **4** plankton

Page 25 **1** **1** pelican **2** puffin **3** oystercatcher **2** **1** false **2** false **3** true **4** false **5** false **6** true

Page 26 **1** **1** sand dunes **2** cave **3** cliffs **4** arch **5** stack **6** ocean **2** **1** coast **2** cliffs **3** sand dunes **4** caves

Page 27 **1** **1** people **2** flag **3** animals **4** plants

Teaching Ideas

See also pages 8–9 for general ideas that you can adapt. Or go to **www.oup.com/elt/teacher/readanddiscover**

READ & TALK Beach Animals
After completing the project, students find out about other beach animals. They can look in other books or the Internet. They can make posters about each animal, using the model on page 28 for support. Students can work in groups, and posters can then be displayed together, organizing them by different types of animals, for example, birds, fish, mammals.

READ & TALK Food Chain Posters
After completing the project, students draw their food chains on a poster and then present them to the class: *[Crabs] eat [starfish] and [starfish] eat [clams].* Posters can then be displayed together.

READ & TALK Which Animal Is It?
Choose a photo of one of the animals from the Reader. Then without saying the animal's name, describe the animal to the class: *This animal lives in ...*; *It has ...*; It eats ... Then ask students to guess which animal it is. Students can then do this in small groups or pairs.

READ & TALK I Spy ...
Find some pictures of beaches from magazines or the Internet. Play *I-Spy* with the pictures. Ask the class to guess the beach item that you have chosen from the picture: *I spy with my little eye, something beginning with ...* Students can then play *I-Spy* in small groups or pairs.

A Beach Collage
Students make a beach collage with beach pictures and/or items collected from a beach (sand, pebbles, shells, etc.). Then they label their collage. Collages can then be displayed together.

1 In the Sky

Subject Area

The Natural World

Topics & Curriculum Links

the sky and space (Science; Geography)
moons, stars, and planets (Science)
day and night (Science)
machines (Science; Technology)
light and energy; electricity (Science)
weather (Science)
space travel (Science; Technology)
shapes (Mathematics)
sizes and measurements (Mathematics)

Vocabulary

transportation; weather; places; colors; shapes; sizes; numbers

Grammar

present simple; *can/can't*; question forms; imperative; adjectives; prepositions

Activities Answers

Page 20 **1** 1 bird 2 sky 3 spacecraft 4 cloud 5 plane 6 rainbow **2** 1 sky, space 2 big 3 rainbow

Page 21 **1** 1 false 2 true 3 false 4 true 5 false **2** 1 moon 2 stars 3 rock 4 fire

Page 22 **1** 1 star 2 Earth 3 sun 4 hot 5 Don't look **2** 1 Earth 2 eyes 3 sun 4 sky 5 electricity

Page 23 **1** 1 Earth 2 night 3 day 4 light 5 sun **2** 1 true 2 false 3 false 4 true

Page 24 **1** 1 stars 2 telescope 3 galaxy 4 photo 5 pattern **2** 1 yellow 2 constellations 3 telescope 4 galaxy

Page 25 **1** 1 Neptune 2 Uranus 3 Saturn 4 Jupiter 5 Mars 6 Earth 7 Venus 8 Mercury **2** 1 Eight 2 solar 3 Saturn 4 one

Page 26 **1** 1 dust 2 mountains 3 rock 4 hole 5 wind 6 breathe **2** 1 Astronauts can go to the moon. 2 Astronauts have space suits. 3 Astronauts breathe air from a tank.

Page 27 **1** 1 space 2 photos 3 planets 4 station **2** 1 planet 2 space station 3 space 4 astronaut 5 people

Teaching Ideas

See also pages 8–9 for general ideas that you can adapt
Or go to **www.oup.com/elt/teacher/readanddiscover**

Stars Research

After reading Chapter 5, students do research, using books or the internet, about famous constellations that they can see in their country. Students can then make a poster about the constellations – they can draw the stars and label them with their names in English.

A Planets Mobile

After reading Chapter 6, students make a simple mobile of the planets, using cardboard and string. They can label the planets. Students can also do research, using books or the internet, about the planets, and they can write simple sentences about the planets. Students can do this in pairs or small groups.

READ & TALK The Sky Where I Live

After completing the project, students present their findings to the rest of the class. They can talk or write about it like this: *On Day 1, the sky is [color]. There are (no) clouds/birds. I can/can't see the sun. I can also see ... On Night 1, the sky is [color]. I can see (no) lights. I can/can't see a moon/stars. I can also see ...*

Sky Collages

After completing the project, students find different pictures of the sky and make sky collages with them. You can divide the class into two groups – one group makes a day collage, the other group makes a night collage. Students then label what they can see in the collages. The collages can then be displayed in class.

READ & TALK Sky Paintings

Students do research, using books or the internet, about famous paintings of skies. Students can then make a poster about a chosen painting. They can talk or write about the painting like this: *This painting is by [name of painter]. It's in the day/at night. The sky is [color]. I can see ... I like/don't like this painting.*

1 Wild Cats

Subject Area

The Natural World

Topics & Curriculum Links

types of wild cat (Science)
climate (Science)
parts of a cat's body (Science)
where wild cats live (Science; Geography)
senses (Science)
what wild cats eat (Science)
baby wild cats and parents (Science)
wild cats in danger (Civics)
sizes and measurements (Mathematics)

Vocabulary

animals; places; parts of the body; food and drink; colors; numbers; sizes

Grammar

present simple; *can/can't*; question forms; imperative; adjectives; prepositions; adverbs

Activities Answers

Page 20 1 1 in holes in the ground 2 in rainforests 3 in snowy mountains **2** 1 big 2 hot 3 fur 4 climb

Page 21 1 1 spots 2 rocks 3 stripes 4 grass **2** 1 true 2 false 3 false 4 true

Page 22 1 1 deer 2 roar 3 tongue 4 bite 5 teeth **2** 1 big 2 four 3 bite 4 tongue

Page 23 1 1 serval 2 lynx 3 ocelot 4 mice **2** 1 ears 2 smell 3 fur

Page 24 1 1 run 2 jump 3 land 4 turn **2** 1 false 2 true 3 true 4 false

Page 25 1 1 claw 2 antelope 3 bird 4 zebra 5 lion 6 snake **2** 1 Some cats eat antelopes and zebras. 2 Big cats can run very fast. 3 The leopard eats snakes. 4 The tiger has sharp claws.

Page 26 1 1 meat 2 mouth 3 milk 4 hunt **2** 1 three 2 one 3 four 4 two

Page 27 1 1 food 2 sell 3 zoo 4 danger 5 skin 6 rainforest **2** 1 Some people cut down trees in rainforests. 2 Some people hunt big cats for their skin. 3 Some zoos protect animals.

Teaching Ideas

See also pages 8–9 for general ideas that you can adapt. Or go to **www.oup.com/elt/teacher/readanddiscover**

READ & TALK A Wild Cat Presentation

After completing the project, students make a poster about a wild cat and then present it to the class. Or students first talk about the wild cat without saying its name, and ask the class to guess the wild cat before showing their poster. Students then display all the posters together, organizing them into different types of wild cat, or where they live. Students can then vote for their favorite cat.

READ & TALK Mystery Wild Cat

Collect big pictures of wild cats, and use a sheet of card to cover the picture except for a very small 'window' that shows a very small part of the picture. Ask students to guess which wild cat it is, from what they can see.

READ & TALK Which Wild Cat Is It?

Choose one of the wild cats from the Reader, and without giving the page number, read out a sentence about it and ask students to guess which wild cat it is. Read out more sentences, one at a time, until students guess the correct wild cat. You can use a point scoring system, for example five points after one sentence, three points after two sentences, etc. Students can then do this in small groups or pairs.

READ & TALK Wild Cats in My Country

Students find out about wild cats in their country. They find out where they live, what they eat, what senses they use, etc. Students then choose one wild cat and make a fact file about it, by answering the questions on page 29 of the Reader, and illustrating it with a photo or drawing. Then students present their wild cat to the class.

Wild Cats Around the World

Students choose a wild cat and find out about where it lives around the world. Then they make a poster showing a picture of the wild cat, and the countries where it lives. Students can use a copy of the world map on page 9 to show the countries where the wild cat lives. Posters can then be displayed together.

1 Young Animals

Subject Area

The Natural World

Topics & Curriculum Links

animals (Science)
animal life cycles (Science)
young animals and parents (Science)
how animals care for their babies (Science)
how young animals stay safe (Science)
food and drink for young animals (Science)
sizes, measurements, and quantities (Mathematics)

Vocabulary

animals; places; daily activities; food and drink; parts of the body; sizes; colors; weather; numbers; time expressions

Grammar

present simple; *can/can't*; question forms; imperative; adjectives; prepositions; adverbs

Activities Answers

Page 20 **1** 1 nest 2 eggs 3 warm 4 hatch **2** 1 doesn't hatch 2 brown 3 hour

Page 21 **1** 1 sea turtle 2 butterfly 3 caterpillar 4 seahorse **2** 1 true 2 false 3 true 4 false

Page 22 **1** 1 an elephant 2 an ostrich 3 a chimpanzee **2** 1 A mother elephant feeds a young elephant. 2 Adult elephants help a young elephant to walk. 3 A mother chimpanzee carries a baby chimpanzee. 4 A mother and father live with a young ostrich.

Page 23 **1** 1 spots 2 pouch 3 caterpillar 4 shark 5 kangaroo 6 ocean The secret word is poison **2** 1 eat 2 kangaroos 3 kangaroo 4 poison

Page 24 **1** 1 seal 2 owl 3 toad 4 tadpole **2** 1 true 2 false 3 false 4 false

Page 25 **1** 1 bear 2 beaver 3 grass 4 branch **2** 1 den 2 lodge 3 dam 4 mud

Page 26 **1** 1 eat 2 hunt 3 fly 4 run **2** 1 Young cheetahs watch their mother hunt. 2 A mother cheetah gives little animals to her young cheetahs. 3 A young eagle learns to fly when it's about ten weeks old.

Page 27 **1** 1 lion 2 larva 3 pupa 4 beetle **2** 1 pride 2 larva 3 pupa 4 adult

Teaching Ideas

See also pages 8–9 for general ideas that you can adapt. Or go to **www.oup.com/elt/teacher/readanddiscover**

READ & TALK A Young Animals Presentation

After completing the project, students make a poster about a young animal and then present it to the class. Or students can first talk about the animal without saying its name, and ask the class to guess the animal before showing their poster. Students can then display all the posters together, organizing them, for example, into young animals that are born from mothers, and young animals that hatch from eggs.

READ & TALK A Young Animals Quiz

Ask the class quiz questions, using facts from the Reader. Ask true/false questions, or questions starting with *What*, *Where*, *When*, etc., or give a definition and ask students to give an answer. Students can work in pairs or small groups. Then in pairs or small groups, students can ask their own quiz questions.

READ & TALK How Babies Are Born

Ask students to say which of these animals hatch from eggs and which animals are born from their mothers: *sea turtle, chimpanzee, butterfly, elephant, ostrich, duck, zebra, seal, toad, bear, beetle, kangaroo, owl, beaver, eagle.* Students can make two lists, and then they can find out about other young animals and add them to the lists. They can also divide the list of animals that hatch from eggs into animals that look like their parents, and animals that don't look like their parents. Students then share their findings with the class.

READ & TALK Young Animals Research

Students find out about other young animals. For each animal, they can answer these questions: *Does it hatch from an egg? Is it born from its mother? Does it look like its parents? Does it live with its parents? Does it drink milk from its mother? Does it eat food? What does it eat? Where does it live? What does it live in?* Students can then present their finding to the rest of the class.

READ & TALK Young Animals Where I Live

Students find out about animals that grow up in the area where they live. They can find out where they live, what they eat, what dangers there are for them, and how they stay safe. Students can use the language on pages 28–29 of the Reader to help them. Then they can present their findings to the class.

Art

Subject Area

The World of Arts & Social Sciences

Topics & Curriculum Links

types of art (Art)
lines and shapes (Mathematics)
places and countries (Geography)
animals (Science)
materials (Science; Technology)
tools (Science; Technology)
museums (Civics)

Vocabulary

types of art; places; countries; parts of the body; artist's equipment; materials; animals; shapes; sizes; colors; weather; numbers

Grammar

present simple; *can/can't*; question forms; imperative; adjectives; prepositions

Activities Answers

Page 20 **1** **1** world **2** shapes **3** mountain **4** animals **5** artist **6** colors **2** **1** Artists **2** art **3** colors **4** like

Page 21 **1** **1** Spain **2** happy **3** boy **4** colors **5** picture **2** **1** picture **2** tree **3** mirror **4** teacher **5** dog

Page 22 **1** **1** lion **2** eyes **3** bird **4** ocean **2** **1** can't **2** can **3** six **4** birds

Page 23 **1** **1** pen **2** draw **3** artists **4** shapes **2** **1** pencil **2** pen **3** boat **4** bedroom

Page 24 **1** **1** purple **2** green **3** red **4** orange **5** blue **2** **1** colors **2** yellow **3** sky **4** stones

Page 25 **1** **1** false **2** true **3** false **4** true **2** **1** sculpture **2** hammer **3** wood **4** goat

Page 26 **1** **1** car **2** fabric **3** beach **4** cans **2** **1** Peru **2** Fabric **3** materials **4** cans

Page 27 **1** **1** museums **2** York **3** Spain, shapes **2** **1** museum **2** books **3** people **4** website **5** shapes

Teaching Ideas

See also pages 8–9 for general ideas that you can adapt. Or go to **www.oup.com/elt/teacher/readanddiscover**

READ & TALK My Favorite Picture

After completing the project activity on page 29 of the Reader, students use their answers to present their favorite picture. Students can record the class results and then make a bar graph showing how many students prefer each picture.

READ & TALK Which Picture Is It?

Choose one of the pictures from the Reader, and without giving the page number, read out a sentence about it and ask students to guess which picture it is. Read out more sentences, one at a time, until students guess the correct picture. You can use a point scoring system, for example five points after one sentence, three points after two sentences, etc. Students can then do this in small groups or pairs.

READ & TALK A Picture Presentation

Ask students to find a copy of a picture of people, animals, or landscapes that they like, and to write about it. They can use the models on pages 5, 6, 7, and 9 of the Reader. Students present their picture to the class. They then display the pictures together, organizing them into pictures of people, animals, and landscapes, etc.

READ & TALK My Picture

Students paint or draw their own picture. Then they talk or write about it like this: *This is ... There is/are ... The [object] is [color]; I like ...* The pictures can then be displayed together and students can vote for their favorite picture.

READ & TALK A Museum Near Where I Live

Ask students to visit a museum near where they live and to answer the following questions: *Where is the museum? What can you see there? What is your favorite painting or sculpture there?* Students then report back to the class.

1 Schools

Subject Area
The World of Arts & Social Studies

Topics & Curriculum Links
daily life (Civics)
places and countries (Geography)
classroom behaviour (Civics)
uniform (Civics)
sports and other hobbies (Civics)
food (Science)
weather (Science)
sizes (Mathematics)

Vocabulary
buildings; places; transportation; school equipment; food; clothes; animals; weather; age; sizes; colors; countries

Grammar
present simple; *can/can't*; question forms; imperative; adjectives; prepositions

Activities Answers

Page 20 **1** 1 bus 2 sled 3 train 4 bicycle 5 car **2** 1 students 2 walk 3 bus 4 school **3** 1 true 2 false 3 true 4 true

Page 21 **1** 1 true 2 false 3 true 4 true **2** 1 school 2 playground 3 city 4 countryside

Page 22 **1** 1 bell 2 bag 3 classroom 4 hallway **2** 1 hallway 2 says 3 books 4 bags

Page 23 **1** 1 teacher 2 books 3 have 4 classes **2** 1 computer 2 giraffe / picture 3 book 4 basketball / physical education class

Page 24 **1** 1 boat 2 food 3 plate 4 tray **2** 1 cafeteria 2 food 3 plate 4 you

Page 25 **1** 1 true 2 false 3 true 4 false **2** 1 shirt 2 skirt 3 sweater 4 tie

Page 26 **1** 1 band 2 soccer 3 vegetables **2** 1 free time 2 friends 3 school 4 play

Page 27 **1** 1 trips 2 zoo 3 animals 4 dinosaur 5 learn **2** 1 students 2 dinosaur 3 teacher 4 zoo 5 museum

Teaching Ideas

See also pages 8–9 for general ideas that you can adapt. Or go to **www.oup.com/elt/teacher/readanddiscover**

READ & TALK How Do You Go to School?
After reading Chapter 1, students do a class survey on how students in the class go to school. They can ask each other: *How do you go to school?* They collect all the information from the class, by listening to each student giving information in turn, or by collecting the class information in a big chart on the board. Then they make a bar chart showing how many students go to school by different transportation.

READ & TALK A New Uniform
After completing the project, students present their new uniform to the rest of the class: *The boys wear ...*; *The girls wear ...* Students then vote for their favorite new uniform.

READ & TALK My Favorites Poster
Students make a poster about their favorite things at school. They can find or draw pictures to decorate the poster. They can write or talk about their favorite things like this: *At school, my favorite subject/sport/food/trip is ...* Then they can present their favorite things to rest of the class.

My School
Students draw a plan of their own school or classroom. Then they label the plan. Students can compare their plans in small groups or pairs, to see if there are any differences.

READ & TALK My Amazing School
Students imagine their own amazing school. They can write and talk about the classes, sports, food, etc. like this: *In my amazing school, we have music lessons every day/ we eat pizza at lunchtime ...* Students can present their school to the rest of the class, and students can vote for the best amazing school.

Electricity

Subject Area

The World of Science & Technology

Topics & Curriculum Links

daily life (Civics)
machines (Science)
electricity in nature (Science)
how we make electricity (Science)
batteries (Science)
how we get electricity (Science)
how electricity moves through materials (Science)
pollution (Science; Civics)
being safe with electricity (Science; Civics)
uses of electricity (Science; Civics)

Vocabulary

household objects; places; daily activities; transportation; machines; materials; sizes; colors

Grammar

present simple; *can/can't*; question forms; imperative; adjectives; prepositions

Activities Answers

Pages 20–21 **1** 1 energy 2 work 3 electricity 4 machines **2** 1 machine 2 bus 3 train 4 car **3** 1 refrigerator 2 stove 3 dishwasher 4 kettle **4** 1 Kettles make water hot. 2 Refrigerators keep our food cold. 3 Stoves cook our food. 4 Washing machines wash our clothes. 5 Dishwashers wash our dishes.

Pages 22–23 **1** 1 lightning 2 sky 3 electric shock 4 sun **2** 1 false 2 false 3 true 4 true **3** 1 Lightning is a type of electricity in the sky. 2 Lightning has lots of energy. 3 Lightning is very, very hot. 4 Lightning can give you an electric shock. 5 An electric shock is when electricity goes into your body. **4** 1 Lightning has lots of energy. 2 Lightning is very, very hot. 3 When you see lightning in the sky, go into your home. 3 An electric shock is when electricity goes into your body. 4 Electricity makes amazing colors in the sky in the Arctic and the Antarctic.

Pages 24–25 **1** 1 coal 2 steam 3 turbine 4 generator 5 electricity **2** 1 We make electricity in power stations. 2 Many power stations use coal to make electricity. **3** 1 power station 2 wind 3 water 4 river 5 steam **4** 1 river 2 turns 3 use 4 wind

Pages 26–27 **1** 1 calculator 2 camera 3 cell phone 4 watch 5 batteries 6 machine **2** 1 cell phone 2 calculator 3 car 4 watch 5 battery 6 camera **3** 1 Most batteries are small. 2 They make electricity for small machines. 3 Some machines use two or more batteries to work. 4 Big batteries make electricity for big machines. **4** 1 small 2 watches 3 car 4 satellites 5 batteries

Pages 28–29 **1** 1 electricity 2 office 3 socket 4 school 5 wires 6 plug **2** 1 true 2 true 3 false **3** 1 Wires take electricity to sockets. 2 We put a plug in a socket. 3 Electricity goes from a socket to a plug. 4 Wires take electricity from a plug to electric machines. **4** 1 We put a plug in a socket to use electricity. 2 Electricity moves in wires./Wires take electricity from one place to another place. 3 We can put one plug in a socket. 4 A socket can get hot and burn when we out too many plugs in it.

Pages 30–31 **1** 1 Electricity 2 metal 3 wires, stations 4 water 5 machine, shock **2** 1 true 2 false 3 true 4 true **3** 1 Plugs have plastic on them. 2 Plastic stops electricity moving to us when we touch a plug. 3 The glass stops electricity moving from wires into a metal pylon. 4 The glass on pylons stops electricity moving to the ground.

Pages 32–33 **1** 1 coal 2 shower 3 electricity 4 pollution 5 lamp 6 bath 7 computer 8 machine **2** 1 Power station make pollution by burning coal. 2 To stop pollution we can turn off lamps, computers, and other machines when we are not using them. We can have a shower, not a bath. **3** 1 wind, water 2 stations, pollution 3 sun 4 panels, pollution

Pages 34–35 **1** 1 wires 2 powder 3 fire 4 kite **2** 1 Don't put electric machines next to water. 2 Firefighters use powder to stop electric machines burning. 3 Don't fly a kite next to electricity wires. **3** 1 It isn't safe to put your fingers in sockets or electric machines. 2 Electricity can move from the socket or the machine to you. 3 Electricity can give you an electric shock. 4 free answers

Teaching Ideas

See also pages 8–9 for general ideas that you can adapt.
Or go to **www.oup.com/elt/teacher/readanddiscover**

READ & TALK An Electricity Presentation

After completing Project 1, students present their posters about being safe with electricity to the rest of the class. Posters can then be displayed together, and students can vote for their favorite poster.

READ & TALK Machines at Home

After completing Project 2, students collect the results from the whole class. They can do this by listening to each student giving their information in turn, or by collecting the information in a big version of the chart on page 37 of the Reader. Students then make a big class display of all the machines at home.

READ & TALK Machines That Use Batteries

Students work in small groups and think of all the machines that use batteries. They make two lists: machines that use big batteries, and machines that use small batteries. Then students share their results with the class and make two big lists.

Stop Pollution!

Students make posters about what we can do to stop pollution. They can use language from pages 16–17 of the Reader and they can illustrate each point. Posters can then be displayed together, and students can vote for their favorite poster.

Power Stations

Students find out about power stations near where they live. They can make a map showing where the places are. On the map, they can write sentences about each power station like this: *This power station is in [name of place]; This power station uses [coal/wind/water] to make electricity.*

Subject Area

The World of Science & Technology

Topics & Curriculum Links

plastic things (Science; Technology)
types of plastic (Science; Technology)
how we make plastic (Science; Technology)
daily life (Civics)
plastic at home (Science; Civics)
plastic waste (Science; Civics)
how plastic can hurt animals (Civics)
recycling plastic (Science; Technology)
making plastic from plants (Science; Technology)

Vocabulary

household objects; toys; materials; places; food and drink; daily activities; transportation; parts of a house; sizes; colors

Grammar

present simple; *can/can't*; question forms; imperative; adjectives; prepositions

Activities Answers

Pages 20–21 **1** 1 bottle 2 pen 3 chopsticks 4 spoon **2** 1 material 2 shapes 3 bottles 4 plastic **3** 1 plastic 2 strong 3 hard 4 soft **4** 1 false 2 true 3 true 4 false 5 false 6 true

Pages 22–23 **1** 1 plastic 2 coil 3 ground 4 liquid 5 pieces 6 factory **2** 1 We can make plastic from oil. 2 We get oil from under the ground. 3 We can get different types of liquid from oil. 4 We use plastic pieces to make plastic things. **3** 1 factory 2 soft; shapes 3 mold; spoon 4 cold; hard 5 spoons

Pages 24–25 **1** 1 bottle 2 juice 3 light 4 water **2** 1 We can buy juice, soda, and water in plastic bottles. 2 We can buy food in plastic wrap. / We can buy sandwiches, salad, and cake in plastic wrap. 3 We use one liter of oil to make four plastic bottles. **3** 1 box 2 food 3 transparent 4 plastic 5 salad 6 cake **4** 1 false 2 false 3 true 4 false

Pages 26–27 **1** 1 door 2 roof 3 pipe 4 window frame **2** 1 There's lots of plastic at home. 2 We use plastic to make many doors. 3 Plastic stops rain getting into our homes. **3** 1 fibers 2 colors 3 curtains 4 plastic 5 make **4** 1 We use plastic fibers to make many carpets, curtains, and clothes. 2 We can make paint from plastic. 3 We use paint on the walls at home. 4 Students' own answers.

Pages 28–29 **1** 1 kite 2 kayak 3 ball 4 bat 5 toys 6 plastic 7 helmet 8 bicycle 9 goggles **2** 1 true 2 false 3 false 4 true 5 false **3** 1 Plastic helps us to be safe when we go outside. 2 Plastic goggles protect our eyes. 3 Plastic pads protect our elbows and knees. 4 Plastic helmets are light and very strong. 5 Plastic helmets don't break. 6 Plastic helmets protect our head. **4** 1 pads 2 elbows 3 head 4 knees 5 helmet 6 goggles

Pages 30–31 **1** 1 throw away; plastic 2 waste 3 burn 4 Pollution **2** 1 ocean 2 animals 3 waste 4 burn 5 pollution 6 bad **3** 1 Some plastic waste goes in the ocean. 2 Many animals live in the ocean. 3 The plastic waste is very bad for the animals. **4** 1 Some plastic things break into small pieces. 2 Animals eat plastic pieces and they get sick. 3 Some animals eat plastic bags and they get sick. 4 Some plastic waste hurts animals.

Pages 32–33 **1** 1 recycle 2 factory 3 fibers 4 pieces **2** 1 We take plastic bottles to a recycling center. 2 We take the bottles to a factory. 3 We break the bottles into small plastic pieces. 4 We use the plastic pieces to make fibers. 5 We use the fibers to make T-shirts. **3** 1 kayak 2 chair 3 T-shirt 4 Playground **4** 1 False 2 True 3 False 4 False

Pages 34–35 **1** 1 oil 2 plants 3 plastic cup 4 plastic bag **2** 1 We use lots of oil to make plastic. 2 We can't make more oil. 3 We use plastic every day. 4 There's too much plastic waste. **3** 1 plastic 2 bottles 3 Recycle 4 plants **4** 1 center 2 new 3 cups 4 today 5 plastic 6 bottles 7 make The secret word is 'recycle'.

Teaching Ideas

See also pages 8–9 for general ideas that you can adapt. Or go to **www.oup.com/elt/teacher/readanddiscover**

READ & TALK Plastic Things

After completing Project 1, students collect the results from the whole class. They can do this by listening to each student giving their information in turn, or by collecting the information in a big version of the chart on page 36 of the Reader. Students then make a bar graph showing how many plastic things they found in their bedrooms, kitchens, and classrooms.

READ & TALK Different Types of Plastic

Students work in small groups to make a chart that lists as many plastic things as they can think of. On the chart they label four columns: *Hard*, *Soft*, *Light*, *Transparent*, and they tick whether the plastic is hard, soft, light, or transparent. Students then collect the results from the whole class and make one big chart. They can also find pictures of the plastic things and label them. The chart and the pictures can then be displayed in class.

READ & TALK A Plastic Quiz

Ask the class quiz questions, using facts from the Reader. Ask true/false questions, or questions starting with *What*, *Where*, *When*, etc. Students can work in pairs or small groups, and they can look for the answers in the Reader. Then in pairs or small groups, students can ask their own quiz questions.

Recycle Your Plastic!

Students make a poster about recycling plastic things and not throwing plastic away. They can use the title: *Recycle Your Plastic!* They write reasons, for example: *There's too much plastic waste. Some people burn plastic waste and this makes pollution. Some plastic waste hurts animals.* Then they illustrate the reasons. The posters can be displayed around the school.

Using Plastic to Make New Things

Ask students to bring in clean plastic waste from home, for example, plastic cups, bottles, cutlery, old CDs. Once students have collected enough plastic waste, they re-use the plastic things to make something new, for example, a piece of art like a collage or sculpture, or something useful, like a pen holder or desk organizer. Alternatively, students can do this at home. The new creations can then be displayed in class and students can vote for the best one.

Subject Area

The World of Science & Technology

Topics & Curriculum Links

weather (Science)
seasons (Science)
the water cycle (Science)
types of wind (Science)
animals (Science)
day and night; light and dark (Science)
geographical features (Science)
states of water (Science)
plants and animals (Science)

Vocabulary

weather; seasons; animals; food; colors; places; daily activities; numbers

Grammar

present simple; *can/can't*; question forms; imperative; adjectives; prepositions; adverbs

Activities Answers

Pages 20–21 **1** 1 sun 2 Earth 3 light 4 heat **2** 1 true 2 false 3 true 4 false **3** 1 sunny 2 seasons 3 warm 4 cold **4** 1 warm 2 winter 3 cold 4 summer

Pages 22–23 **1** 1 cloud 2 rain 3 river 4 ocean 5 plants 6 animals **2** 1 false 2 false 3 true 4 true **3** 1 rivers 2 oceans 3 sunny 4 sky 5 clouds 6 rain

Pages 24–25 **1** 1 Some clouds are gray. 2 Some clouds are white. 3 Gray clouds have many raindrops. 4 White clouds don't have many raindrops. **2** 1 sky 2 gray 3 white 4 sun 5 hot 6 light **3** 1 clouds 2 umbrella 3 earth 4 storm 5 raindrops 6 lightning Secret word: season **4** 1 big 2 big 3 make 4 hot

Pages 26–27 **1** 1 When is water in clouds ice? When it's very cold in the sky. 2 What is ice when it falls to Earth? It's snow. 3 What is snow when it melts? It's water. 4 Where does the water go? It goes into the ground and rivers. **2** 1 When it's very cold in the sky, water in clouds is ice. 2 When ice falls to Earth, the ice is snow. 3 When snow falls on warm ground, the snow melts. 4 Then the snow is water again. **3** 1 snow 2 skiing 3 cloud 4 house 5 mountain 6 car **4** 1 false 2 false 3 true

Pages 28–29 **1** 1 up 2 cold 3 down **2** 1 air 2 sun 3 sky 4 cold 5 down **3** 1 flag 2 breeze 3 hurricane 4 tree 5 house 6 sky **4** 1 A breeze blows slowly. 2 A hurricane blows fast. 3 It can blow down trees and houses.

Pages 30–31 **1** 1 false 2 true 3 false **2** 1 leaves 2 fruit 3 bird 4 monkey 5 frog 6 minibeasts **3** 1 Many animals live in warm, wet rainforests. 2 Monkeys eat nuts and fruit. 3 Birds eat minibeasts and nuts and fruit, too. 4 Small frogs drink raindrops on big leaves. **4** 1 It is warm and wet all year. 2 They live in trees. 3 They eat minibeasts, nuts and fruit.

Pages 32–33 **1** 1 Arctic, Antarctic 2 water 3 plants 4 ice, snow 5 animals **2** 1 ocean 2 tree 3 nuts 4 ice 5 fish 6 seal **3** 1 swim 2 fish 3 fat 4 warm **4** 1 They eats lots of fish. 2 They get very fat.

Pages 34–35 **1** 1 When it's sunny, people can get hot. 2 When it's rainy, people can get wet. 3 When it's sunny, people wear a hat. 4 When it's rainy, people use an umbrella. **2** 1 Many buildings have windows with shutters. 2 The shutters stop the heat and light going in. 3 When it's rainy, people can get wet. 4 Rain falls off roofs. **3** 1 umbrella 2 cloud 3 light 4 rain 5 breeze 6 storm 7 snow 8 sun 9 lightning 10 hurricane

Teaching Ideas

See also pages 8–9 for general ideas that you can adapt. Or go to **www.oup.com/elt/teacher/readanddiscover**

READ & TALK The Water Cycle

After reading Chapter 2, give students a blank copy of a water cycle diagram, showing only the ocean and the mountain. Ask students to color the ocean and the mountain, draw and color the river, stick cotton balls on for clouds, draw lines for evaporation, and stick on pieces of blue paper or glitter for the rain falling. Students label the water cycle. Students then practise telling each other how the water cycle works, using the model on page 9 of the Reader.

A Clouds Collage

After reading Chapter 3, students find the names of other types of cloud. They can look in other books or on the Internet. Then they draw or find picture of the clouds and label them. The pictures can then be displayed together, with all the same types of cloud together.

READ & TALK Sunny and Rainy Posters

After reading Chapter 8, students make posters showing what people do when it's sunny and when it's rainy. They can talk and write about it like this: *When it's sunny/rainy, many people wear .../people can ...* Students make separate posters for 'sunny' and 'rainy' and then all the sunny posters and all the rainy posters can be displayed together.

A Temperatures Bar Chart

When doing Project 1, students can also take and record the temperature every day. Then they can make a bar chart showing the daily temperatures.

READ & TALK My Weather Card

After completing Project 2, students write a more detailed weather card for where they live. They can write and talk about the weather in each month/season like this: *In [month/season] it's sunny/rainy/windy.* Students can draw or find pictures to decorate the card.

2 Your Body

Subject Area
The World of Science & Technology

Topics & Curriculum Links
parts of the body (Science)
what your body can do (Science)
senses (Science)
sports and exercise (Civics; Science)
daily life (Civics)
protecting your body (Science; Civics)
healthy food (Science; Civics)
quantities and measurements (Mathematics)

Vocabulary
daily activities; parts of the body; weather; sizes; transportation; clothes; numbers

Grammar
present simple; *can/can't*; question forms; imperative; adjectives; prepositions; adverbs

Activities Answers

Pages 20–21 **1** 1 skin 2 sweat 3 hair 4 dirt **2** 1 body 2 touch 3 cold 4 dirt 5 water **3** 1 true 2 false 3 false 4 false 5 true **4** 1 Your skin helps you to touch things, and to know when things are hot or cold. 2 Hair on your arms and legs stands up when you're cold, and stops your body getting too cold. 3 You can wash every day to protect your skin and hair.

Pages 22–23 **1** 1 bone 2 skeleton 3 elbow 4 knee 5 joints 6 body **2** 1 Bones 2 skeleton 3 joints 4 Bones **3** 1 A baby has small bones. 2 Bones grow and they make you big and tall. 3 Your bones stop growing when you are about 20 years old. 4 There are 206 bones in your body. **4** 1 baby 2 under 3 you 4 small 5 tall 6 wear

Pages 24–25 **1** 1 Muscles pull your bones. 2 Muscles help you to ride a bicycle 3 Muscles help you to row a boat. 4 There are more than 600 muscles in your body. **2** 1 muscles 2 arms 3 legs 4 bones 5 joints 6 body **3** 1 jumping 2 swimming 3 running 4 walking 5 dancing 6 riding a bicycle **4** 1 You can do exercise every day. 2 No, the heart is a type of muscle. 3 Exercise makes your heart strong. 4 free answers

Pages 26–27 **1** 1 Your eyes help you to see the world around you. 2 They open and close many times every day. 3 When your eyes blink, they wash dirt out of your eyes. **2** 1 You blink about 15 times every minute. 2 Your eyes close to help you to sleep. 3 You can wear sunglasses on sunny days. **3** 1 listen to 2 listen for 3 ears 4 bad **4** 1 listen 2 music 3 sunny 4 blinking 5 loud 6 hear 7 wash 8 eyes 9 close 10 ears Secret word: sunglasses

Pages 28–29 **1** 1 nose 2 food 3 breathe **2** 1 After exercise, people breathe fast. 2 Your nose and mouth take air into your body. 3 People breathe 15 times every minute. 4 After exercise, people can breathe 40 times every minute. **3** 1 false 2 false 3 true 4 true **4** 1 smell 2 bite 3 teeth 4 breathe 5 food 6 nose

Pages 30–31 **1** 1 speak 2 read 3 brain 4 eyes 5 muscles 6 hands **2** 1 see 2 brain 3 move 4 brain **3** 1 Your brain works all day and at night. 2 At night your brain makes you breathe. 3 At night your brain makes your heart work. 4 Your brain remembers things that you learn. 5 Wear a helmet when you ride a bicycle. **4** 1 day 2 bicycle 3 work 4 hot 5 muscles 6 eyes

Pages 32–33 **1** 1 fingers 2 breathe 3 sick 4 mouth 5 germs 6 cut 7 skin 8 touch **2** 1 sick 2 breathe 3 eat 4 fingers 5 body **3** 1 soap, fingers 2 hands, eat 3 touch animals 4 sneeze 5 tissue, wastebasket

Pages 34–35 **1** 1 strong 2 sleep 3 food 4 water 5 protect 6 grow **2** 1 free answers 2 Good food helps your bones to grow. 3 free answers **3** 1 There's lots of water in your body. 2 You lose water when you go to the toilet. 3 You lose water when your body makes sweat. 4 Drink water every day. **4** 1 food 2 water 3 doctor 4 dentist 5 exercise 6 sleep

Teaching Ideas

See also pages 8–9 for general ideas that you can adapt. Or go to **www.oup.com/elt/teacher/readanddiscover**

READ & TALK My Body Poster
After completing Project 1, students present their poster to the rest of the class. Posters can then be displayed together, organizing them into different parts of the body.

READ & TALK An Exercise Graph
After completing Project 2, students collect all the information and make a graph for the whole class. They can do this by listening to each student giving information in turn, or by collecting the class information in a big chart on the board. Then they make a bar chart showing the different activities and the number of students that do them, to find the most popular exercise. They can talk or write about the chart like this: *A lot of/some/a few students swim/dance/run/walk/ride a bicycle/ride a skateboard. The favorite exercise is swimming/dancing/running/walking/riding a bicycle/riding a skateboard.*

READ & TALK Which Part of the Body?
Choose one of the parts of the body in the Reader, and without saying its name, read out one sentence about it and ask students to guess which part of the body it is. Read out more sentences, one at a time, until students guess the correct part of the body. Students can then do this in small groups or pairs.

READ & TALK Protect Your Body!
Students design a poster about what to do to protect your body. They can draw pictures and talk or write about them like this: *Wash every day! Brush your teeth after breakfast and after dinner! Don't eat lots of candy! Do exercise every day! Don't listen to loud music! Wear a helmet when you ride a bicycle! Eat food that's good for you. Drink lots of water!* etc. Students can also talk or write about how they protect their own body, like this: *I wash every day. I brush my teeth after breakfast and after dinner. etc.*

READ & TALK Simon Says
Play *Simon Says* using different parts of the body, for example: *Simon says touch your nose/head/hair/arm/foot, etc. Move your elbow/knee, etc.* Students can then play the game in small groups, taking in turns to give the instructions.

Subject Area
The Natural World

Topics & Curriculum Links
animals and their homes (Science)
parts of an animal's body (Science)
shapes (Mathematics)
plants (Science)
seasons (Science)
weather and climate (Science)

Vocabulary
animals; plants; places; parts of the body; sizes; shapes; colors; seasons; weather

Grammar
present simple; *can/can't*; present continuous; question forms; imperative; adjectives; prepositions; adverbs

Activities Answers

Pages 20–21 **1** **1** **fur** **2** bird **3** spider **4** tree **5** tiger **6** flowers **2** **1** animals **2** camouflage **3** hide **4** body **5** color **6** stripes **3** **1** camouflage **2** Tigers **3** feathers **4** animals **5** hide **4** **1** Animals use camouflage to hide. **2** Tigers have fur on their body. **3** Stripes help a tiger to hide. **4** Birds have feathers on their body. **5** Some spiders hide on flowers.

Pages 22–23 **1** **1** monkey **2** seal **3** ice **4** leaf **5** caterpillar **2** **1** true **2** false **3** true **4** false **3** **1** color **2** hiding **3** brown **4** rainforests **5** swim **6** ice **4** **1** The mother harp seal is gray. **2** The mother harp seal swims in the water. **3** The baby harp seal is white. **4** The baby harp seal lives on ice.

Pages 24–25 **1** **1** fox **2** feathers **3** summer **4** winter **5** grouse **6** fur **2** **1** brown – grouse in summer **2** white – grouse in winter **3** white – Arctic fox in winter **4** brown – Arctic fox in summer **3** **1** summer **2** feathers **3** brown **4** white **5** snow **6** melts **4** **1** Some animals have white fur or feathers to hide in snow. **2** The grouse is brown in summer. **3** The Arctic fox is white in winter. **4** The snow melts in summer.

Pages 26–27 **1** **1** hide **2** hunt **3** lion **4** grass **5** gazelle **2** **1** true **2** false **3** true **4** false **5** false **6** true **3** **1** Lots of animals live in Africa. **2** Some animals hide in the grass. **3** A lion hides so gazelles can't see it. **4** A gazelle hides so lions can't see it. **5** Gazelles can run very fast. **4** **1** grass **2** hunt **3** use **4** Gazelles **5** baby

Pages 28–29 **1** **1** fish **2** mirror **3** ocean **4** scales **5** stones **6** coral **2** **1** frogfish – next to coral **2** flounder – at the bottom of the ocean **3** hatchet fish – in the deep ocean **4** leafy sea dragon – next to plants **3** **1** The frogfish lives next to coral. **2** The flounder looks the same as the stones. **3** The hatchet fish has shiny scales. **4** The leafy sea dragon looks the same as a plant. **4** **1** The frogfish looks the same as the coral. **2** The flounder lives at the bottom of the ocean. **3** The hatchet fish lives in the deep ocean. **4** The leafy sea dragon looks the same as a plant.

Pages 30–31 **1** **1** pattern **2** beetle **3** stripes **4** sand **5** coral **2** **1** false **2** true **3** true **4** false **5** true **3** **1** The beetle is yellow. **2** A bird comes to eat the beetle. **3** The beetle gets a new color and a new pattern. **4** The beetle looks the same as a ladybug. **5** The bird goes away. **6** The beetle is yellow again. **4** **1** brown **2** body **3** camouflage, pattern **4** beetle **5** ladybugs

Pages 32–33 **1** **1** rainforest **2** insects **3** hole **4** frog **5** leaf **6** gecko **2** **1** an insect **2** holes **3** rainforest **4** leaf **3** **1** The katydid looks the same as a leaf. **2** The leaf insect has holes in its body. **3** The frog lives in a rainforest. **4** The leaf gecko uses camouflage. **4** **1** animals **2** leaf **3** wind **4** holes **5** camouflage **6** gecko

Pages 34–35 **1** **1** Stick insects look the same as a stick. **2** Lithops plants look the same as stones. **3** Some caterpillars look the same as a snake. **4** Lots of animals use camouflage to hide. **2** **1** insects **2** plants **3** stones **4** animals **5** caterpillar **6** snake **3** **1** The caterpillar looks the same as a snake. **2** The caterpillar has two circles on its body. **3** When the caterpillar is scared, it makes the circles big. **4** **1** ice **2** pattern **3** summer **4** coral **5** fur **6** feathers **7** leaf **8** scales **9** grass **10** winter

Teaching Ideas

See also pages 8–9 for general ideas that you can adapt. Or go to **www.oup.com/elt/teacher/readanddiscover**

READ & TALK A Camouflage Presentation
After completing Project 1, students present their posters to the rest of the class. Posters can be displayed together, organized by the type of camouflage the animal uses. Students can then vote for their favorite poster.

READ & TALK Camouflage Research
After completing Project 2, students find out about how other animals use camouflage. Then they share their findings with the class.

READ & TALK Which Animals Is It?
Choose one of the animals from the Reader, and without saying its name, read out one fact about it and ask students to guess which animal it is. Read out more facts, one at a time, until students guess the correct animal. You can use a point scoring system, for example five points after one fact, three points after two facts, etc. Students can then do this in small groups or pairs.

READ & TALK A Camouflage Quiz
Ask the class quiz questions, using facts from the Reader. Ask true/false questions, or questions starting with *What*, *Where*, *When*, etc., or give a definition and ask students to give an answer. Students can work in pairs or small groups. Then in pairs or small groups, students can ask their own quiz questions.

READ & TALK Where Is the Animal?
Find pictures of camouflaged animals and ask the class to find and name the animals. Students then find more pictures, and in turn they ask the rest of the class to find and name the animals. The pictures can then be displayed together, organized by the type of camouflage.

Earth

Subject Area

The Natural World

Topics & Curriculum Links

places and countries (Geography)
physical features of Earth (Geography)
land and water (Science)
weather and climate (Science)
plants and animals (Science)
quantities and measurements (Mathematics)
time (Mathematics)

Vocabulary

transportation; places; animals; weather; countries; seasons; numbers

Grammar

present simple; *can/can't*; question forms; imperative; adjectives; prepositions; adverbs

Activities Answers

Pages 20–21 **1** 1 ocean 2 forest 3 mountain 4 cloud 5 river 6 desert **2** 1 planet 2 space 3 water 4 oceans **3** 1 lakes 2 land 3 day 4 goes 5 one **4** 1 On Earth, there's land and water. 2 There's water in lakes and rivers. 3 Earth is a planet. 4 Millions of people live on Earth. 5 Earth is our home.

Pages 22–23 **1** 1 cliffs 2 land 3 valley 4 canyon **2** 1 mountain 2 millions 3 amazing 4 ocean 5 snowy 6 forest **3** 1 live 2 mountains 3 canyon 4 are 5 fall **4** 1 under our feet 2 be snowy mountains 3 make deep valleys 4 a deep valley 5 canyon in Peru 6 Earth are old

Pages 24–25 **1** 1 melt 2 waves 3 lake 4 waterfall 5 rain **2** 1 true 2 false 3 true 4 true 5 false 6 false **3** 1 cliff 2 oceans 3 wind 4 swim **4** 1 On Earth, there's water in rivers, lakes, and oceans. 2 Most rivers come from mountains. 3 Most rivers go to the ocean. 4 A river makes a waterfall when it comes to a cliff.

Pages 26–27 **1** 1 sun 2 equator 3 Earth **2** 1 hot 2 deserts 3 water 4 rivers 5 sunny **3** 1 There are a lot of hot places near the equator. 2 Monument Valley is in the USA. 3 It's hot and sunny in Monument Valley. 4 When it's hot, the lungfish makes a hole in the soil. 5 Near the equator, the light from the sun is strong. **4** 1 There are a lot of hot places near the equator. 2 Monument Valley is in the USA. 3 The weather is very hot and sunny. 4 The lungfish makes a hole in the soil when it's hot.

Pages 28–29 **1** 1 dog 2 sled 3 penguin 4 electricity **2** 1 cold 2 lots of 3 dark 4 can't 5 Antarctic 6 friends **3** 1 cold 2 sun 3 snow 4 winter 5 stand 6 colors **4** 1 In the Arctic, people have sleds and dogs. 2 In the Antarctic, there are penguins. 3 The Arctic and the Antarctic are very cold places. 4 Electricity from the sun makes amazing colors in the sky.

Pages 30–31 **1** 1 rainforest 2 plants 3 umbrella 4 insects **2** 1 cold 2 rainy 3 hot 4 weather 5 monsoon 6 summer **3** 1 isn't 2 rainy 3 monsoon 4 wet 5 rainforests 6 are **4** 1 is the rainy time 2 and rainy in rainforests 3 animals in rainforests 4 can eat insects

Pages 32–33 **1** 1 soil 2 volcano 3 cave 4 animals 5 water 6 rock **2** 1 false 2 true 3 false 4 true 5 true 6 true **3** 1 find 2 rock 3 volcano 4 people 5 Water 6 caves **4** 1 Rock is under the soil. 2 Rock is millions of years old. 3 When a volcano erupts, hot rock comes out. 4 You can see amazing rock in caves.

Pages 34–35 **1** 1 place 2 fish 3 animals 4 are 5 dark 6 new **2** 1 There are millions of plants in the ocean. 2 Trenches are long, deep canyons. 3 Some animals make light. 4 It's very cold and dark in the deep ocean. **3** 1 Trenches are long, deep canyons in the ocean floor. 2 It is cold in the deep ocean. **4** 1 space 2 lake 3 dark 4 mountain 5 deep 6 desert 7 river 8 cave 9 rainforest 10 forest 11 light; Planet Earth

Teaching Ideas

See also pages 8–9 for general ideas that you can adapt. Or go to **www.oup.com/elt/teacher/readanddiscover**

READ & TALK An Amazing Places Quiz

After completing Project 2, students describe an amazing place: *It's a [hot/cold/dry/wet] place. It's a ... It's in ...* Then other students guess which place it is. Students can do this in small groups or pairs.

READ & TALK A True/False Quiz

Using sentences from the Reader, read out some true facts and change some to make them false. Ask students to say if the facts are true or false. Students can then do the same activity in small groups or pairs.

Places on Earth

Students work in small groups and choose a physical feature of Earth, for example, mountains, deserts, lakes, rivers. Using other books or the Internet, they find examples from around the world, and make a list of the names and countries. They can use a copy of the world map from page 9 to show where the places are.

Land and Water

Students look through the Reader and find words for the two categories 'Land' and 'Water'. They can display the words in two lists, for example: *Land: forest, mountain, desert ..., Water: ocean, river ...* Then students can share their words with the class and collect all the words on the board.

READ & TALK My Island

Give groups of students a plastic tray and plasticine to make their own island. They can make mountains, volcanoes, rivers, lakes, cliffs, etc. They can also make features under the ocean, and then add water to flood the areas around their island. Students then present their island to the rest of the class. They can talk and write about their island like this: *On my island there is a .../there are ...* Students then vote for their favorite island.

Farms

Subject Area
The Natural World

Topics & Curriculum Links
types of farms (Geography)
animals and animal products (Science; Geography)
plants and crops (Science; Geography)
food (Science)
machines (Science; Technology)
weather (Science)
sizes, measurements, and quantities (Mathematics)

Vocabulary
places; weather; seasons; animals; food; clothes; sizes; numbers

Grammar
present simple; *can/can't*; present continuous; question forms; imperative; adjectives; prepositions; adverbs

Activities Answers

Pages 20–21 **1** 1 bread 2 wool 3 eggs 4 meat 5 vegetables 6 fruit **2** From Crops: vegetables, bread, fruit; From Animals: milk, wool, eggs, meat **3** 1 true 2 false 3 true 4 false 5 true 6 false **4** 1 On some farms there are crops. 2 Farmers work every day. 3 Crops are plants that we eat. 4 Wool comes from animals.

Pages 22–23 **1** 1 rice 2 wheat 3 strawberries 4 sugar cane 5 bananas 6 pineapples **2** 1 Rice 2 flour 3 nine 4 Soft fruits **3** 1 weather, soil 2 hot 3 cool 4 water **4** 1 A lot of sugar comes from a crop called sugar cane. 2 Wheat grows in big fields. 3 You can make bread, pasta, and cakes with flour. 4 They cut rice terraces into mountains.

Pages 24–25 **1** 1 First farmers plow the fields. 2 Then they plant seeds. 3 Then they give the plants water. 4 Later, they cut the crops. **2** 1 They help farmers. machines 2 When the farmers cut or pick the crops. harvest 3 It's a crop. cotton 4 Farmers put them on their crops. chemicals 5 Farmers grow them with no chemicals. organic crops **3** 1 machines 2 plow 3 seeds 4 plants 5 hot 6 organic **4** 1 Yes, they do. 2 Chemicals stop animals eating crops. 3 Crops with no chemicals. 4 Cotton comes from big white flowers on the cotton plant.

Pages 26–27 **1** 1 cheese 2 meat 3 milk 4 butter 5 cream 6 yogurt **2** 1 They live in fields in spring and summer. 2 They eat lots of grass. 3 Some cattle live in barns in winter. **3** 1 grass 2 hay 3 milk 4 ranch **4** 1 true 2 true 3 false 4 false

Pages 28–29 **1** 1 We use a sheep's fleece to make wool. 2 We use wool to make hats. 3 A lamb drinks milk. **2** 1 lamb 2 fleece 3 grass 4 wool **3** 1 wool, meat, milk 2 outside 3 milk, grass 4 grass **4** 1 We get meat from sheep. 2 Sheep have a woolen coat. 3 We make socks from wool. 4 A lamb drinks its mother's milk.

Pages 30–31 **1** 1 feathers 2 duck 3 chicken 4 goose 5 ostrich 6 eggs **2** 1 F 2 FR 3 FR **3** 1 geese, chickens, ducks, ostriches 2 meat, eggs, feathers 3 pillows, quilts 4 eggs, meat, feathers **4** 1 They are called poultry. 2 They live outside. 3 They keep ostriches for eggs, meat, and feathers. 4 It's as big as 40 chicken eggs.

Pages 32–33 **1** 1 lake 2 ocean 3 fish 4 food 5 tank 6 net **2** 1 lakes 2 big 3 sell 4 good **3** 1 Farmers feed fish so they grow big. 2 When fish are big, farmers can sell them. 3 Lots of salmon come from fish farms. **4** 1 nets 2 lakes 3 tanks 4 ocean 5 sell

Pages 34–35 **1** 1 false 2 true 3 true 4 false 5 false **2** 1 trees 2 seed pods 3 seeds 4 vanilla 5 skin **3** 1 Crops: bread, cotton, rice; Cattle: milk, meat; Sheep: wool; Poultry: feathers, eggs **4** 1 chocolate, cacao 2 butter, milk 3 bread, wheat 4 feathers, birds

Teaching Ideas

See also pages 8–9 for general ideas that you can adapt. Or go to **www.oup.com/elt/teacher/readanddiscover**

READ & TALK My Farm
After completing Project 1, students present their farm to the rest of the class: *My farm is called ... Here is the [building]. I grow [crops]. I keep [animals].* Students can then vote for the best farm.

READ & TALK Animal Fact Files
After completing Project 2, students make more fact files about animals on farms. They can write and talk about them like this: *[Animals] eat [food]. They live in ... We get [food].* Students can draw or find pictures to decorate the fact files. They can then be displayed in class, organized by type of animal.

READ & TALK A Farm Near Where I Live
Students do research, using books or the internet, about a farm near where they live. They can draw a picture or take a photo of the farm, and they can talk or write about the farm like this: *This farm is big/small. On this farm, there are animals. There are [animals]. We get [product] from [animals]. On this farm there are crops. There are [crops]. We get [product] from [crops].*

READ & TALK Where Does It Come From?
Ask students to make a list of the things that they wear, eat, drink, and use every day. Collect the ideas on the board. Then ask students to say where the products come from – from plants or from animals. For the products that don't come from plants or animals, you could introduce *minerals* or just say *other things*.

Crops Research
Students do research, using books or the internet, about crops – where different crops grow, what the plants look like, and what products are made from the crops. They can make fact files about the crops, and they can talk or write about the farm like this: *This crop is called ... It grows ... We get ... from ...* The fact files can then be displayed in class, organized by type of crop, type of products, or where in the world the crop grows.

In the Mountains

Subject Area

The Natural World

Topics & Curriculum Links

how mountains form (Science)
volcanoes (Science)
living in the mountains (Geography; Civics)
animals (Science)
plants (Science)
ice and snow (Science)
climate and countries (Geography)
weather and seasons (Science)
mountain sports (Civics; Technology)
safety in the mountains (Civics)
sizes and measurements (Mathematics)

Vocabulary

places; food and drink; animals; parts of the body; plants; sports; transportation; sizes; shapes; weather; seasons; continents

Grammar

present simple; *can/can't*; question forms; imperative; adjectives; prepositions; adverbs

Activities Answers

Pages 20–21 **1** 1 mountains 2 volcano 3 Earth 4 hole 5 million 6 rock **2** 1 places 2 moves 3 mountain 4 millions **3** 1 mountains 2 hole 3 rock 4 dangerous **4** 1 Mountains are very old. 2 Mountains are very high. 3 Mount Everest is 8,850 meters high. 4 Earth has a crust. 5 Earth's crust moves very, very slowly. 6 Under Earth's crust there's hot rock.

Pages 22–23 **1** 1 terraces 2 road 3 food 4 electricity **2** 1 mountain 2 car 3 animal 4 house 5 water 6 rice **3** 1 roads 2 animals 3 have 4 rocks 5 near 6 terraces **4** 1 Some people in the mountains don't have a car. 2 Some people in the mountains don't have electricity. 3 People use rocks from the mountains to make their homes. 4 People make terraces and grow food

Pages 24–25 **1** 1 snow leopard 2 nest 3 paw 4 climb 5 alpaca 6 fur **2** 1 false 2 true 3 false 4 true 5 true 6 false **3** 1 walk 2 wings 3 South America 4 fur **4** 1 They live in the mountains in Asia. 2 They live in the mountains in Asia, North America, Africa, and Europe. 3 They live in the mountains in South America. 4 free answers

Pages 26–27 **1** 1 rain 2 leaves 3 needles 4 snow 5 bud 6 roots **2** 1 needles 2 can't 3 snow 4 water **3** 1 Conifers are a type of tree. 2 Conifers don't have big leaves. 3 Very high in the mountains, it's very cold and windy. 4 Plants have long roots. 5 There isn't much rain high in the mountains. 6 Some mountain plants make strong buds. **4** 1 There are conifers in the mountains. 2 Conifers have small needles. 3 Conifers can grow in cold places. Some plants can live very high in the mountains.

Pages 28–29 **1** 1 river 2 glacier 3 slowly 4 crevasse 5 avalanche 6 fall **2** 1 Snow 2 falls 3 moves 4 slowly **3** 1 ice 2 weather 3 dangerous 4 falls **4** 1 A glacier is a river of ice. 2 Glaciers move very, very slowly. 3 In some glaciers, there are big crevasses. 4 Crevasses are dangerous.

Pages 30–31 **1** 1 rope 2 wheel 3 raft 4 helmet **2** 1 climber 2 strong 3 bike 4 great 5 sport 6 rocks **3** 1 rope 2 arms 3 have 4 summer 5 snow 6 rocks **4** 1 Rafting is a great summer sport. 2 Rafts are very strong. 3 Rafts can go over rocks. Mountain bikes have strong wheels. 5 Do you have a mountain bike?

Pages 32–33 **1** 1 children 2 snow shoes 3 skis 4 walk 5 sled **2** 1 false 2 true 3 true 4 true 5 true 6 false **3** 1 skiing 2 school 3 snow 4 difficult 5 walk **4** 1 Sledding is a great sport. 2 You can go very fast on a sled. 3 Do you like walking? 4 You can walk in snowshoes. 5 Snowboarders fall in the snow.

Pages 34–35 **1** 1 helicopter 2 map 3 compass 4 bread 5 cheese 6 water **2** 1 You can get lost in the mountains 2 Helicopters come and help people. 3 Take food and water when you walk in the mountains. 4 Don't drink water from a river. 5 Be careful in the mountains **3** 1 It's snowy. 2 It's sunny. 3 It's cloudy. 4 It's rainy. **4** 1 warm clothes 2 chocolate 3 water 4 fruit 5 bread 6 compass 7 cheese 8 map

Teaching Ideas

See also pages 8–9 for general ideas that you can adapt. Or go to **www.oup.com/elt/teacher/readanddiscover**

READ & TALK A Mountain Poster

After reading Chapter 8, students make a poster to illustrate what to take when walking in the mountains. They can talk and write about it like this: *When you walk in the mountains, take [food/drink/clothes]. It's good to eat [food].* Posters can then be displayed together.

READ & TALK A Mountain Animal Presentation

After completing Project 1, students present their mountain animal posters to the rest of the class. Posters can then be displayed together, and students can vote for their favorite poster.

READ & TALK Mountain Fact Files

After completing Project 2, students find out about other mountains and write more fact files. Fact files can then be displayed together.

READ & TALK A Mountains Quiz

Ask the class quiz questions, using facts from the Reader. Ask true/false questions, or questions starting with *What*, *Where*, *When*, etc. Students can work in pairs or small groups, and they can look for the answers in the Reader. Then in pairs or small groups, students can ask their own quiz questions.

Big Mountains Around the World

Give students a list of big mountains around the world, for example, Mount Everest (Himalayas), Mauna Loa (Hawaii), Aconcagua (Argentina), Mount Logan (Canada), Mont Blanc (France/Italy), Kilimanjaro (Tanzania), Mount Cook (New Zealand), Hallasan (South Korea), Mount Etna (Italy). Then ask students to find out where the mountains are and how high they are. Students can use a copy of the world map on page 9 to show where the mountains are, and they can write their names and how high they are

2 Cities

Subject Area

The World of Arts & Social Studies

Topics & Curriculum Links

cities and countries (Geography)
places in cities (Geography)
buildings and homes (Geography; Civics)
daily life (Civics)
tourism (Geography; Civics)
transportation (Technology)
jobs (Civics)
time (Mathematics)
sizes, measurements, and quantities (Mathematics)

Vocabulary

places; buildings; transportation; time; jobs; sizes; numbers

Grammar

present simple; *can/can't*; present continuous; question forms; imperative; adjectives; prepositions

Activities Answers

Pages 20–21 **1** 1 city 2 buildings 3 street 4 bus 5 taxi 6 people **2** 1 work 2 big 3 cities 4 people **3** 1 streets 2 buses 3 cities 4 eleven 5 going 6 taking **4** 1 It's seven o'clock in the morning. 2 People are going to work. 3 It's a new day in the city. 4 Every day new people come to the city.

Pages 22–23 **1** 1 store 2 museum 3 school 4 mall **2** 1 family 2 friends 3 window 4 photo 5 restaurant 6 people **3** 1 mall 2 stores 3 restaurants 4 mall 5 old 6 city **4** 1 lots of buildings 2 schools, and stores 3 very tall buildings 4 with your family 5 in store windows 6 cars, and buses

Pages 24–25 **1** 1 ship 2 harbour 3 bridge 4 river 5 ocean **2** 1 false 2 true 3 false 4 true 5 true 6 false **3** 1 ocean 2 buildings 3 big 4 come **4** 1 It's in Australia. 2 Yes, it is. 3 There are nice apartments and restaurants. 4 It's in the USA. 5 Yes, there is. 6 It has more than 400 bridges.

Pages 26–27 **1** 1 tourists 2 guide 3 rickshaw 4 park 5 lake 6 boat **2** 1 tourist 2 parks 3 guide 4 walk 5 ride 6 rickshaw **3** 1 There are lots of things to do in a city. 2 You can go to a museum. 3 In Udaipur there's a big lake. 4 You can ride on the lake in a boat. 5 Udaipur is a city in India. **4** 1 It's fun to be a tourist. 2 You can go to a park. 3 You can ride on a bus. 4 It's good to walk around a city. 5 You can take photos of buildings.

Pages 28–29 **1** 1 house 2 apartment 3 playground 4 children 5 tree 6 flowers **2** 1 small 2 people 3 balconies 4 nice 5 San Francisco **3** 1 USA 2 old 3 stairs 4 offices **4** 1 Many homes in cities are small. 2 People live in houses or apartments. 3 San Francisco is an old city. 4 Berlin is in Germany.

Pages 30–31 **1** 1 taxi driver 2 telephone 3 police officer 4 computer **2** 1 morning 2 salesclerk 3 store 4 nurse 5 teacher 6 thousand **3** 1 work 2 use 3 people 4 people 5 stores 6 people **4** 1 people go to work 2 work in offices 3 work in stores 4 salesclerks help us 5 work in a city

Pages 32–33 **1** 1 pollution 2 tracks 3 tram 4 train 5 car 6 station **2** 1 false 2 true 3 true 4 false 5 true 6 false **3** 1 can't 2 car 3 cities 4 don't 5 Thousands 6 station **4** 1 It's great to walk in a city. 2 Many people use transportation. 3 Cars make pollution. 4 Trams run on tracks.

Pages 34–35 **1** 1 park 2 theater 3 restaurant 4 movie 5 afternoon 6 evening **2** 1 It's three o'clock. 2 It's seven o'clock. 3 It's twelve o'clock. 4 It's eleven o'clock. **3** 1 It's fun to go to the park in the afternoon. 2 Some parks have a lake. 3 There are lots of things to do in the evenings. 4 People meet their friends in restaurants. 5 Some people work at night. 6 At twelve o'clock at night, many people are at home. **4** 1 Some people go to the park. 2 You can ride in boats on the lake or talk to friends. 3 Some people go to the theatre, a movie or a restaurant. 4 Taxi drivers and police officers work at night.

Teaching Ideas

See also pages 8–9 for general ideas that you can adapt.
Or go to **www.oup.com/elt/teacher/readanddiscover**

READ & TALK A City Quiz

After completing Project 1, students take turns to ask the rest of the class to guess their city. Students can ask the questions on page 36 of the Reader, to try to guess the city. This can be done as a whole class, in small groups, or pairs.

City Fact Files

After completing Project 1, students make fact files about other cities. Students can draw or find pictures to decorate the fact files. They can then be displayed in class, organized by country or continent.

READ & TALK I-Spy

Find some pictures of cities from magazines or the internet. Play *I-Spy* with the pictures. Ask the class to guess what you have chosen from the picture: *I spy with my little eye something beginning with ...* Students can then play *I-Spy* in small groups or pairs, using magazine pictures, or pictures from the Reader.

READ & TALK A City in My Country

Students do research, using books or the internet, about a city in their country. Then they design a poster for tourists, to promote the city. They can find or draw pictures of the city, and they can talk or write about the city, using sentences in the Reader as models.

READ & TALK A New City

Students design a new city. First they decide what it's called, where it is, if it's big or small, what you can do in the city, etc. Then they draw a map of it, and they can talk or write about it like this: *This city is called [name]. It's a big/small city. You can ... etc.* Students can then vote for their favorite city.

Jobs

Subject Area

The World of Arts & Social Studies

Topics & Curriculum Links

types of job (Civics)
where people work (Civics)
when people work (Civics)
making things (Science; Technology)
helping people (Civics)
working with animals (Civics)
jobs with animals (Civics)

Vocabulary

jobs; places; colors; clothes; transportation; food; animals; parts of a house; household objects; seasons

Grammar

present simple; *can/can't*; present continuous; question forms; imperative; adjectives; prepositions

Activities Answers

Pages 20–21 **1** 1 office 2 flight attendant 3 telephone 4 firefighter 5 plane 6 computer **2** 1 are 2 outside 3 planes 4 help 5 hot **3** 1 People use computers in an office. 2 Firefighters wear a uniform. 3 People make roads outside. 4 Flight attendants work on planes. 5 Firefighters go into very hot buildings. **4** 1 orange 2 body 3 road 4 building 5 office 6 hot

Pages 22–23 **1** 1 chef 2 tourists 3 city 4 park 5 restaurant **2** 1 true 2 false 3 true 4 false 5 true **3** 1 Cities are big and busy. 2 Lots of people work in cities. 3 You can take a bus in a city. 4 Bus drivers do a job. **4** 1 People work in stores, parks and libraries. 2 Chefs cook the food in restaurants. 3 Tour guides work with tourists. 4 You can take a bus or a tram.

Pages 24–25 **1** 1 fish 2 animals 3 crops 4 market 5 ocean 6 ground The secret word is 'farmer'. **2** 1 rice 2 fish 3 metal 4 bananas 5 coal 6 olives **3** 1 outside 2 grow 3 animals 4 ocean 5 metal **4** 1 Farmers work in the countryside. 2 Some farmers keep animals. 3 Rice and bananas are crops. 4 Some people catch fish from the ocean. 5 Miners work under the ground.

Pages 26–27 **1** 1 camera 2 buildings 3 hands 4 machine 5 cell phone 6 factory **2** 1 true 2 false 3 true 4 false **3** 1 people 2 hands 3 factories 4 new 5 windows 6 make **4** 1 Lots of people make things. 2 Many people work in factories. 3 It takes a long time to make a building. 4 Some people make machines.

Pages 28–29 **1** 1 parents 2 danger 3 police officer 4 teacher 5 doctor 6 ambulance **2** 1 children 2 Nurses 3 help 4 people **3** 1 Firefighters and ambulance workers help people. 2 Parents help children at home. 3 Doctors help sick people. 4 Teachers help children at school. **4** 1 Doctors and nurses help sick people. 2 Teachers help children at school. 3 Police officers help people. 4 Police officers, firefighters and ambulance workers can be in danger when they do their job.

Pages 30–31 **1** 1 zoo 2 danger 3 animals 4 pelican 5 vet **2** 1 sick 2 vets 3 jobs 4 dogs **3** 1 Lots of people work with animals. 2 Some vets help wild animals. 3 Guide dogs help people who can't see. 4 Some vets work in animal parks. **4** 1 Some vets work in zoos. 2 Some people help animals in danger. 3 People teach animals to do jobs. 4 Guide dogs help people who can't see.

Pages 32–33 **1** 1 sleep 2 day 3 night 4 train 5 store 6 taxi **2** 1 You sleep at night. 2 Many doctors work at night. 3 Some stores are open all night. 4 Railway workers work on train tracks. 5 Cities are busy at night. 6 People can go home in taxis. **3** 1 jobs 2 nurses 3 factories 4 train 5 cities 6 busy **4** 1 food 2 movie 3 food 4 friend 5 busy 6 people 7 sleep

Pages 34–35 **1** 1 movie 2 dancing 3 soccer musicians **2** 1 false 2 false **3** 1 Some people make movies. 2 The actors act in the movie. 3 The camera operator uses the camera. 4 The director tells people what to do. **4** 1 Musicians play instruments. 2 Actors, camera operators and directors make movies. 3 Actors act in movies. 4 Students' own answers.

Teaching Ideas

See also pages 8–9 for general ideas that you can adapt. Or go to **www.oup.com/elt/teacher/readanddiscover**

READ & TALK My Favorite Job Presentation

After completing Project 1, students present their favorite job to the rest of the class. Students then vote for their favorite job.

READ & TALK Job Cards

After completing Project 2, students find out about other jobs and make more job cards. The jobs cards can then be displayed together, organized into jobs inside or outside, in the day or at night, with people or animals, etc.

READ & TALK Which Job Is It?

Choose one of the jobs from the Reader, and without saying its name, read out one fact about it and ask students to guess which job it is. Read out more facts, one at a time, until students guess the correct job. You can use a point scoring system, for example five points after one fact, three points after two facts, etc. Students can then do this in small groups or pairs.

READ & TALK Jobs Where I Live

Students make a list of all the jobs that people do in their local area. They can choose an area near the school, or where they live. They draw a plan of the area and then they write the different jobs on the plan. Plans can then be displayed together.

READ & TALK A Job Interview

Ask students to interview someone they know about their job. If the person speaks English, students can ask these questions: *What is your job? Do you work inside or outside? Do you work in the day or at night? Do you have a uniform? Do you work with people or animals? Do you work for money? Do you like your job?* Alternatively, students can ask the questions in their own language. Students then write or talk about their findings like this: *[name] is a [job]. He/She works inside/outside. He/She works in the day/at night. He/She wears/doesn't wear a uniform. It's... He/She works with animals/people. He/She works/doesn't work for money. He/She likes/doesn't like his/her job.*

Oxford Read and Discover

Series Editor: Hazel Geatches • CLIL Adviser: John Clegg

Oxford Read and Discover graded readers are at six levels, for students from age 6 and older. They cover many topics within three subject areas, and support English across the curriculum, or Content and Language Integrated Learning (CLIL).

Available for each reader:
- Audio CD Pack (book & audio CD)
- Activity Book

Teaching notes & CLIL guidance: **www.oup.com/elt/teacher/readanddiscover**

Subject Area / Level	The World of Science & Technology	The Natural World	The World of Arts & Social Studies
1 300 headwords	• Eyes • Fruit • Trees • Wheels	• At the Beach • In the Sky • Wild Cats • Young Animals	• Art • Schools
2 450 headwords	• Electricity • Plastic • Sunny and Rainy • Your Body	• Camouflage • Earth • Farms • In the Mountains	• Cities • Jobs
3 600 headwords	• How We Make Products • Sound and Music • Super Structures • Your Five Senses	• Amazing Minibeasts • Animals in the Air • Life in Rainforests • Wonderful Water	• Festivals Around the World • Free Time Around the World
4 750 headwords	• All About Plants • How to Stay Healthy • Machines Then and Now • Why We Recycle	• All About Desert Life • All About Ocean Life • Animals at Night • Incredible Earth	• Animals in Art • Wonders of the Past
5 900 headwords	• Materials To Products • Medicine Then and Now • Transportation Then and Now • Wild Weather	• All About Islands • Animal Life Cycles • Exploring Our World • Great Migrations	• Homes Around the World • Our World in Art
6 1,050 headwords	• Cells and Microbes • Clothes Then and Now • Incredible Energy • Your Amazing Body	• All About Space • Caring for Our Planet • Earth Then and Now • Wonderful Ecosystems	• Food Around the World • Helping Around the World